D1078390

MEANING FORM

.ᴏ for Bronze, ᴄ ᴏ.
Gold Medal Candidates
(The Speaking of Verse and Prose)
and ALAM Recital Diploma Candidates

by Paul Ranger

OBERON BOOKS
LONDON

First published in 1995 in association with the London Academy of
Music and Dramatic Art, by Oberon Books Ltd.
(incorporating Absolute Classics),
521 Caledonian Road, London N7 9RH
Tel: 020 7607 3637/Fax: 020 7607 3629
e-mail: oberon.books@btinternet.com

Reprinted with corrections 2000

A catalogue record of this book is available from the British Library.

ISBN: 1 870259 74 2

Cover design: Andrzej Klimowski

Cover typography: Richard Doust

Printed in Great Britain by Antony Rowe Ltd, Reading.

PAUL RANGER

Paul Ranger studied at the Guildhall School of Music and Drama, the College of St Mark and St John, Chelsea, Bristol University and Southampton University.

Alongside acting and directing he has run evening and short courses for adults as well as teaching disabled children. He has been head of an inner-city CE primary school near to Tower Bridge. Later he was made an Adjunct Professor of California State University. Latterly he was Head of the Faculty of Drama, Theatre and Television at King Alfred's University College, Winchester.

He is Chairman of the Society of Teachers of Speech and Drama and editor of *Speech & Drama,* an assessor in drama for Southern Arts and the Arts Council, a director of theatre courses for the Association for Cultural Exchange, a lecturer for the National Trust, University of the Third Age and Inscape Fine Art Tours and a writer of books and articles on performance and theatre history.

He is a member of the Board of Examiners at LAMDA.

FURTHER WORKS BY PAUL RANGER

Experiments in Drama

The Lost Theatres of Winchester

A Masterguide to *She Stoops to Conquer*

A Masterguide to *The School for Scandal*

Terror and Pity Reign in Every Breast

Theatre in the Cotswolds
(in conjunction with Anthony Denning)

A Catalogue of Strolling Companies:
The Ongoing Theatre in Newbury

Performance

The Georgian Theatres of Hampshire

From the Restoration to the Romantics

Under Two Managers: the everyday life of the Thornton/
Barnett circuit of Theatres, 1785-1853

Theatrical entries in the
New Dictionary of National Biography

CONTENTS

INTRODUCTION

To The Teacher

Readership and aims

This book has been written to help candidates preparing for the LAMDA Bronze, Silver and Gold Medal examinations in the Speaking of Verse and Prose and the LAMDA Associate Recital Diploma. Although it is intended mainly for teachers and senior students, in order that selected sections may be used directly by all medal and diploma candidates it is addressed throughout to the student. The book is not intended to replace the teacher, but to be a complementary aid.

A small amount of theoretical information is to be found here; however the book principally provides practical advice on giving a polished performance. Voice training exercises are not included; they are very important and a different LAMDA publication deals with vocal development. In these pages I have used for convenience an inclusive 'he' in referring to both candidates and examiners; however, I should explain that many girls and women take the examinations and women serve on the Board of Examiners.

Selectivity

The book is not designed to be read straight through like a novel. The various skills required for different parts of the examinations are to be found in separate chapters for easy reference. Often material overlaps from one chapter to another and it is recommended that the index is used in order to find all of the material on a specific subject.

Further study

Each chapter contains lists of books for further study. It is not necessary for candidates to read all of these. A choice may be made of one or two from each list in order to follow up personal interests or to gain further information as required. Articles in

Speech & Drama are occasionally recommended; backnumbers of this journal may be obtained from Miss P Charteris, 8 Colebrook Road, Southwick, Brighton BN42 4AL.

The syllabus

The details of the examinations listed above are set out in the current LAMDA syllabus which should be consulted in conjunction with this work.

A word of thanks

I must acknowledge the help and ideas I have received from my fellow examiners and from the numerous candidates I have met. A special word of thanks must go to Shaun McKenna, for his encouragement and many practical suggestions.

Paul Ranger
Oxford 2000

1

LET'S HAVE A PERFORMANCE!

PROJECTING YOUR WORK

As an examiner I'm sometimes surprised by a candidate. He (or she) has come along to the examination having carefully learnt the words of the selected pieces. These are then said, usually in a standing position, clearly, with some hint of their meaning but without the ring of personal conviction. Furthermore the whole of the candidate's attention is fastened on remembering the lines he has to say with the result that he is not making any communication with me; I get the impression that between us there is a great barrier. If I crept out of the room the candidate would continue manfully with his recitation and the absence of an audience would not make any difference. Obviously something is wrong. I had hoped to see a performance but instead I have been left with the dull thud of impersonal words.

That word 'performance' is an extremely important one. Every candidate should regard himself as a performer, someone who is going to interest and entertain the examiner because he is eager to share himself and his prepared work with an audience. In an examination the audience is restricted to either one or, in the case of the diploma, two people; nevertheless you have in each examiner a representative audience. The fact that the member of this audience has occasionally to write notes should not put you off your stride. An examiner has to work with a divided attention but he is well aware of your contribution.

It is imperative for a successful performance that you project your work. This means more than making your voice travel to the listener although that is part of the technique.

The meaning also must be relayed. To do this successfully you use the performance devices available such as modulation, contact, stage presence and visual presentation. Remember, the examiner wants to be captivated by what you have to share with him and is looking for performance quality in your work. You can never, therefore, merely repeat words, although you may do so clearly. You are more than just the postman: you are the voice of the writer whose work you are interpreting. For a few minutes only you can give the content of his work and something of his personality to the audience. Therefore it is important to have mastered not only the meaning but also the tone of the writing: if, for example, you don't notice that the tone of a remark is satirical and speak it mindful only of the surface meaning, then you have distorted the author's intention. The responsibility of conveying the author's message affects your interpretation of the text; you are going to make a personal response to it whilst remaining faithful to the purpose of the writer. This is very difficult to achieve and when the various kinds of text are later considered I want to return to this point.

Although you are speaking words that have been written by a poet, author or dramatist, possibly many years ago, another imperative as a performer is to speak these words with immediacy or spontaneity. Freshness is a marvellous gift: when listening to a great performer one feels that the words spoken are breathed onto the air for the very first time. This can be achieved in your own performance by reliving the thoughts which prompt the words; you are also moved by them and this emotion is responsible for giving sympathetic colouring to your voice. How false the result is if you merely adopt a sad or a longing voice ('putting in the expression') without the necessary feeling underpinning your speaking!

If you have ever stood in the wings of a theatre watching a professional company perform, you will be amazed by the dynamism which is generated on stage. We often talk about relaxation in performance with the result that dynamism becomes forgotten. You need to discover this within yourself during your rehearsals and lessons. Try this very simple exercise:

- stand in a corner of a large room; make sure that your shoulders and neck are relaxed; let your arms hang from your shoulders
- look straight to the front and be aware of the balance of your head on your neck; from the small of your back allow your spine to grow so that you become fractionally taller
- fill your lungs with air and walk alertly across the diagonal of the room

Instantly you begin to experience your own reserves of dynamism.

Relaxation is a complementary alternative to dynamism and this plays its part in your performance. Sometimes physical repose and a total ease of voice are necessary. The change from dynamism to relaxation is not made suddenly. One swims through a sea of interchange from one to the other much of the time and this becomes fascinating to watch and listen to.

In mastering the art of performance you must also learn to look at the audience. I once asked a small girl why she gazed at the ceiling rather than at me as she spoke her poems: 'My teacher says if I look at you, it will make me laugh!' she replied. Not at all. If you look at the examiner in a friendly and open manner, it is a help in making contact with him. Contact is partly a matter of will: you want to interest your audience and this determination helps you to do so.

BODY AND SPACE

Sometimes a candidate forgets that a performer in an examination is more than a disembodied voice. He is a person who can be seen. This means that the visual aspects of the recital are also important. Luckily nowadays most candidates realise that it is not necessary to adopt a formal standing posture in order to speak verse and prose. It may be that a piece full of action (a poem such as *The Diverting History of John Gilpin* by William Cowper is an obvious example) is best spoken standing but there are reflective or lyrical pieces in which a seated position not only helps the speaker to relax and enjoy the work but also the audience is prepared to receive the writing in the spirit in which it was first conceived. *The Oxen* by Thomas Hardy is an example in which the seated candidate can mirror the group of farm workers who:

> ...sat in a flock
> By the embers in hearthside ease.

Contrasts between pieces are important and a change of posture, at its simplest the change from standing to sitting, reinforces the contrast. But there are other positions which may be used as long as the one chosen is appropriate to the piece performed. It is also important to remember that whatever posture we adopt, breathing must not be impeded. However, an unsuitable standing position can be just as much of an impediment to this as any other.

Work towards visual variety, as well as vocal, in planning your recital. Avoid giving two pieces in the same part of the room when you can vary your performance space. Remember, too, to make sure that you are in a good light: it is awkward for the examiner to see you, for instance, if you place yourself against a window to perform.

Carefully plan your use of space. The examiner sits behind a table; your performance area is in front of him. Make sure that there is a divide between yourself and the audience. Too close a proximity with a performer makes the viewer uncomfortable and the overall performance becomes difficult to appreciate. Compare this 'no man's land' with the orchestra pit in an old theatre. Such a divide helps you to establish your own realities in your own world. You may be speaking a Shakespeare sonnet and in doing so you are creating an Elizabethan world in which love is seen more formally than today and expressed in an elaborate word pattern. This formality will affect not only your own speaking, but also your posture and maybe your gesture. For this to be appreciated a certain amount of space is required to act as a 'frame' to your performance which in turn helps the audience to focus on you and what you are conveying.

One way to tackle the challenge of performance space is to imagine a carpet about eight feet by eight feet on the floor of the examination room and determine that you will adjust your work to this space. This can be a help in planning the work but you need to be flexible in the transfer from rehearsal room to examination room. As well as maintaining the actor-audience divide, do make sure that you leave a margin of space between yourself and the side walls. Often candidates look as though they wished they could merge with the plaster on the wall so near do they get to it. The further away from the examiner you stand ('up-stage' in theatre terminology) the more isolated or important you make yourself appear: use this to your advantage. But again, don't press yourself into the back wall or limit the whole of your performance to the up-stage.

What has been written indicates that when you come into the examination room you need to plan the way in which you are going to use the available space. Luckily a few moments elapse whilst the examiner enters details on your report sheet and so you have a brief time in which to make your decisions. Please don't ask the examiner, 'Where do you want me to stand?': this indicates that you have not completed your planning.

THE CONFIDENCE TO PERFORM

Preparation is important. One of the wisest things you can do is to make sure that you are completely secure in your texts: know them so thoroughly that nothing can come between your concentration and the word. Then you can give your entire energy to the business of communication. Having said that, though, it would be foolish not to acknowledge that at times one's memory blanks. If this happens in your examination, quietly say 'Prompt'. A thorough knowledge of your words will ensure that you have confidence both in yourself and in your material. Confidence is a great help in making effective communication; indeed, making connections is one of life's challenges. During the brief span of your examination you are connecting with the examiner-audience and if this is successful, the wonderful amalgam of a shared enthusiasm takes place. True performance is made of such moments.

WHAT SHALL I WEAR?

I once adjudicated the sonnet class at a festival at which the competitors, mostly girls, wore jeans and tee shirts. They seemed quite surprised when I told them that their dress was not appropriate for speaking this artificial, formal poetry. 'Wear what the selected pieces demand,' is the most succinct advice that can be given. It should be easy to move in: boys in school blazers or men in suits rarely do themselves full justice as these often get in the way of performance and hide the candidate rather than reveal him. A practice skirt can often be very useful for a female candidate. This is ankle length and dignified if well made. Furthermore, it can easily be removed revealing underneath something suitable for a second selection if this is required.

FURTHER READING

Ranger, P V, *Performance* (1990)

2
SPEAKING POETRY

MAKING A CHOICE

Have you ever been in love? If so, you will know that when you were first attracted by your partner you discovered an affinity between you. With the barriers down, you shared enthusiasms and you were interested in everything that you could discover about your lover's personality – the merest shrug or grunt had a depth of meaning and fascination not appreciated by anyone else. It's the same with choosing a poem to recite: you must truly love the selected piece. Something about it attracts you even before you fully fathom the meaning, expressed by C Day Lewis as 'to be able to enjoy before we can learn to discriminate'. This means that the verse enthralls you as you devote time to wrestle with its meaning. The implication of this is that the piece is neither the shortest nor the simplest that you can find but rather complexity in the writing makes it interesting to work on over a period of time. In addition to the meaning you must grapple with tone, atmosphere, form, historical and literary context and weave all of these threads into a unified example of speaking.

A poem is like a dress, too. 'That just isn't me!' is the cry from the fitting room when a dress fails to match a personality. It's the same with choosing a poem. There must be something in you that makes you the right person to say a particular poem. Gender plays a part in the choice. Some poems can never be spoken with complete sympathy by a man; and others a woman would be foolish to try. A few poets (Ted Hughes comes to mind) have a masculine way of writing which creates hurdles for a woman speaker. Within this male set there are some poems which are highly sophisticated as well as satirical: much of Alexander Pope's work would fall into this category.

A person whose great virtue is his cheerfulness and open disposition would not make a good speaker for the brittle and sometimes devious quality found in Pope.

As I listen to a candidate, I am occasionally aware that the wrong voice is speaking the text. It does make a difference whether a poem is spoken by a tenor or a bass voice, a soprano or a contralto. The pitch and timbre of the voice can unlock vocalised emotional responses which may or may not be appropriate. A wise drama teacher, Dorothy Heathcote, once pointed out that students (of any age) should be helped to recognise their strengths and develop these. This is particularly true in speaking. You need to know the kind of voice you have, the range of emotion that can be expressed truthfully and easily through it, the kind of writing which appeals and whether you can convey this with sincerity and style.

THE SPEAKER'S RAPPORT WITH THE POET

Key work: *To a Friend with a Religious Vocation* by Elizabeth Jennings

I would like to use Elizabeth Jenning's poem *To a Friend with a Religious Vocation* as an illustration. This consists of a verse letter written to a person about to become a nun by a close friend who has an understanding of this vocation, but realises it is not for her.

> Thinking of your vocation, I am filled
> with thoughts of my own lack of one. I see
> Within myself no wish to breed or build
> Or take the three vows ringed by poverty.
>   And yet I have a sense,
> Vague and inchoate, with no symmetry,
> Of purpose. Is it merely a pretence,
>
> A kind of scaffolding which I erect
> Half out of fear, half out of laziness?

The fitful poems come but can't protect
The empty areas of loneliness.
      You must know what you do,
So that mere breathing is a way to bless.
Dark nights, perhaps, but no grey days for you.

Your vows enfold you. I must make my own;
Now this, now that, each one empirical.
My poems move from feelings not yet known,
And when the poem is written I can feel
      A flash, a moment's peace.
The curtain will be drawn across your grille.
My silences are always enemies.

Yet with the same convictions that you have
(It is but your vocation that I lack),
I must, like you, believe in perfect love.
It is the dark, the dark which draws me back
      Into a chaos where
Vocations, visions fail, the will grows slack
And I am stunned by silence everywhere.

The context indicates that the 'I' in the poem is Elizabeth Jennings herself (remember that the 'I' of a poem is sometimes fictitious) and the content is a deep and confidential conversation, by means of the letter, between the two women, all of which suggests that the poem would be best spoken by a woman.

The speaker is wrestling with her own vocation as a writer, but this has not the clearly mapped ways of the convent life; instead the work entails a tentative empirical approach. Both vocations are frightening:

    It is the dark, the dark that draws me back
      Into a chaos where
    Vocations, visions fail, the will grows slack...

In order to make a response to it a person who chose to speak this poem would need to possess a sympathetic understanding of the religious life and also an insight into the difficulties and successes of the life of a writer. Furthermore the speaker would need to have a sympathy with a poet who has had more than her fair share of illness and nervous prostration. Here the speaker's age is important. Many a younger candidate would not yet have had the time nor suffered the stresses of life to gain the depth of experience expressed in *To a Friend*. So the performer of this poem is a very special kind of person!

THE HISTORICAL AND LITERARY BACKGROUND

Key work: *Tarantella* by Hilaire Belloc

A poem does not exist in a void. It has a literary pedigree and a historical background and when these are carefully researched one's speaking of the poem becomes authoritative. Both of these shape, in part, the poet's style and candidates taking the Silver and Gold Medal examinations are expected, according to the syllabus, to be able to discuss with the examiner the style of the writing. Let us take Hilaire Belloc's poem *Tarantella* as a case study.

> Do you remember an Inn,
> Miranda?
> Do you remember an Inn?
> And the tedding and the spreading
> Of the straw for bedding,
> And the fleas that tease in the high Pyrenees,
> And the wine that tasted of the tar,
> And the cheers and jeers of the young muleteers
> (Under the vine of the dark verandah)?
> Do you remember an Inn, Miranda,
> Do you remember an Inn?
> And the cheers and the jeers of the young muleteers
> Who hadn't got a penny,
> And who weren't paying any,
> And the hammer at the doors and the din?
> And the Hip! Hop! Hap!

Of the clap
Of the hands to the twirl and the swirl
Of the girl gone chancing,
Glancing,
Dancing,
Backing and advancing,
Snapping of the clapper to the spin
Out and in –
And the Ting, Tong, Tang of the Guitar!
Do you remember an Inn, Miranda?
Do you remember an Inn?
Never more;
Miranda,
Never more.
Only the high peaks hoar:
And Aragon a torrent at the door.
No sound
In the walls of the Hall where falls
The tread
Of the feet of the dead to the ground.
No sound:
But the boom
Of the far Waterfall like Doom.

The speaker's knowledge of the background to the poem will affect the way in which he speaks the verse. Let me highlight three points:

- *Tarantella* first appeared in a book of poems by Belloc in 1923. Although Belloc was born in France, he was educated at Birmingham and Oxford. After university he worked as a professional journalist with the result that his style is not only that of an educated man but is also terse and entertaining. This is evident in *Tarantella* and suggests that the speaking must be direct and to the point.

- The speaker must avoid a false romanticism about foreign locations. Travel ran in Belloc's blood: he made his way across France, Italy and over the

Pyrenees. Writing about these travels he expressed his opinion of one inn he stayed at in the mountains a number of times: 'El Plan has a Posada called the Posada of the Sun but it is not praised; nay it is detested by those who speak from experience'. Often I've listened to the poem spoken as if the inn were paradisical instead of a rough hostelry.

- Names in a poem help to determine its tone. Who is Miranda? It seems to me that two interpretations are possible here. When the poem later became popular Belloc claimed that he chose the name because of its rhythm and sound. On the one hand the name may be that of a young woman travelling companion and there may be a tenderness in Belloc's use of it. On the other hand the poet usually made his long walks either alone or with a male companion and it has been suggested by A N Wilson in his biography of Belloc that the name refers to the Duke of Miranda, a London diplomat. If you opt for this possibility, the tone of the poem will be different: it then praises male comradeship.

The poem was written when Belloc was about fifty. The loss of friends at death's hand is obliquely stated in the final section: in a poem in which music and dancing have played a prominent part silence overtakes, giving value to the rumble of the distant waterfall.

Let us consider now several points about the literary conventions:

- Belloc obviously uses a dance rhythm in the poem, a popular ploy of a number of writers at the time; Edith Sitwell's *Facade Suite* is a well-known example. In Italy a large venomous spider is found, the tarantula. It was believed that a man bitten by one of these would start to dance like a maniac as the poison made his nerves highly strung. Composers wrote tarantellas, giving an indication of the puppet-like movements of the afflicted person. It is these musical rhythms Belloc employs and in the speaking, the metre becomes of greater importance than it would in other types of verse.

- However, it is important to remember that the meaning must also be communicated. As we can expect from a journalist the diction (or choice of words) is based on that of everyday conversation, a series of reminiscences, again a popular poetic device.

- Belloc has broken away from the well-established conventional forms, allowing the rhythm and the tenor of what he has to say to dictate the shape of the poem. Sometimes occasional end-rhymes make the pattern plain to a listener; at other times his ear is teased by the use of rhymes within the line:

> And the CHEERS and the JEERS of the young muleTEERS

At one stage the poem thins down so that the rhyming word forms the line:

> ... of the girls gone chancing
> Glancing,
> Dancing...

Both the internal rhymes and the thinning of the poem indicate a rising pace and force in the speaking when the text is interpreted vocally.

FORM, MEANING AND TONE

In looking at *Tarantella* I have started to think about form; it impinges on a great many of our thoughts about poetry. 'Form' relates to the structure and shape of the poem and is concerned with such matters as:

- the number of lines either in the complete poem or each stanza

- the arrangement of the rhyming scheme

- the employment of a metrical pattern

If we were making a literary study of poetry there would be a great deal more to say about each of these. However, I merely want to make some observations about the way in which verse speakers might consider form.

THE SHAPE OF THE POEM

Key work: *Verse* by Walter Savage Landor

One of the simplest arrangements of lines into verses is the four line stanza. I use the brief poem *Verse* by Walter Savage Landor as an illustration.

> Past ruined Ilion Helen lives,
> Alcestis rises from the shades.
> Verse calls them forth; 'tis verse that gives
> Immortal youth to mortal maids.
>
> Soon shall oblivion's deepening veil
> Hide all the peopled hills you see,
> The gay, the proud, while lovers hail
> These many summers you and me.

'What does this mean?' is probably your first response. The meaning, in fact, can only be suitably told through the verse and my paraphrasing in continuous prose is crude. I imagine that Landor is seated in front of a picture showing a classical landscape (perhaps this could be one of Poussin's paintings) and in it are people such as the beautiful Helen of Troy and Alcestis whom great love called back to life from the grave. Landor says that verse is responsible for perpetuating the memory of such immortals and through poetry all similar young maidens may be made immortal. However, time and forgetfulness (Landor's 'oblivion') – death in another word – will in time hide away most of the inhabitants in his imagined landscape.

Now to the speaking. A pause between stanzas is sometimes neglected. In a longer poem with more stanza pauses the various lengths of this pause would have to be considered. In a fast moving narrative poem the pause would be short indeed. In contrast, many a stanza pause prepares for a change of mood. That is so here. The first verse is a description of an idyllic scene. A different mood overtakes the second verse; one is conscious that with the passing of time decay spreads. The writing is tinged with unmentioned death. It is the stanza pause which prepares the listener for this variation and in that pause an emotional change must overtake the speaker, coming from his heart, not simply from his voice.

The rhyming scheme of each verse is the frequently used pattern *abab*. To what extent does a speaker draw attention to the rhyme? The simplicity of the structure here is such that very little notice need be taken; in fact Landor places some of his important words at the beginning of a line. However, the final 'you and me' is highly important, not only as the line ending but also as the termination of the poem, leaving the listener with the knowledge that we today are the present, but temporary, immortals. When making a termination to a poem, judge whether this is just a matter of emphasis or whether a slowing down is necessary. The content and the rhythm of the poetry tend to tell the discerning which is the most appropriate.

It is worth pointing out that Landor ties his lines together in several ways:

- in the first line of stanza 1 the three L repetitions succeed in doing this:

  past ruined iLion heLen Lives

- he uses a complete word, 'verse', in each half of the third line:

  VERSE calls them forth; 'tis VERSE that gives

- and in the last line there is the repeated sound of MORTAL and IMMORTAL, two meanings in opposition

- in stanza 2, second line, the repetition of the H delightfully implies a zephyr blowing through the landscape

  Hide all the peopled Hills you see

- and the long vowel sounds of the first line in this stanza help to stress the alteration of mood:

  sOOn shall oblivion's dEEpening vEIl.

- this implies the slightest change of pace – slower – in the speaking

- there is the same effect in the final line through the use of 'yOU and mE' combined with the sibillants (S and Z sounds) in 'theSE many SummerS'

METRE AND RHYTHM

When working on the metre of a poem, feel the regular heart beat in each line. This is strong in *Verse* where there are four beats to the line, obvious in the second line of the first stanza:

alCEStis RISes FROM the SHADES.

Another way of stating this would be to say that each line of the poem is divided into four feet, each foot containing a stressed syllable, preceded by an unstressed:

/alCES/tis RIS/es FROM/ the SHADES/

Each foot in this /weak STRONG/ pattern is termed an 'iamb'. A change in the regularity of line two occurs in the third line:

VERSE calls/ them FORTH/ 'tis VERSE/ that GIVES/

The iamb at the beginning of the line has been reversed and instead of being the established /weak STRONG/ foot it becomes /STRONG weak/. Combined with the next foot the metrical pattern becomes a choriamb:

/STRONG weak/ weak STRONG/

The effect in speaking is for the words to be given a slight thrust forward as if the poet is eager at the beginning of a line to get on with his story.

In addition to the four feet running through each line there is the merest hint of a pause, felt rather than stated when you are speaking the poem, which occurs in the middle of the line. This is known as a caesural pause. In the third line of stanza 1 Landor places a punctuation mark on the caesura:

Verse calls them forth;* 'tis verse that gives

but in the two preceding lines the presence of the caesura dividing the lines into two is more subtle:

Past ruined Ilion * Helen lives,
Alcestis rises * from the shades.

Feel this pause but, unless there is a mid-line punctuation mark, don't punctuate the line yourself. The great value of the caesural pause, wrote Hilaire Belloc to the poet Ruth Pitter, is that 'it gives infinite variety to a repeated rhythm'.

A number of the line ends are punctuated by either a full stop or a comma and there are three line ends at which no punctuation appears. The full stops indicate that this is a suitable point at which a breath may quietly be taken. Sometimes a breath is necessary at a comma but avoid this if possible. What, though, happens to the lines that are not end-stopped? The reason for the lack of punctuation is, of course, that the sense runs straight through one line and on to the following:

Soon shall oblivion's deepening veil
Hide all the peopled hills you see...

The speaker has a problem. It is necessary to carry the sense from one line to another and he could do this without a pause. The objection to this is that he is not speaking continuous prose but a poem divided into lines and it is important that the pattern of the lines is given to the listener. The solution adopted by many people is known as the 'suspensory pause'. It consists of fractionally lengthening the last syllable of the unpunctuated line and then travelling to the next line giving the first word a slight push forward. These are the mechanics of the technique. It is important that the technique does not draw attention to itself. This remark refers to all mechanical techniques: they are the unseen servants in the transmission of the text.

THE INTENTION OF THE POET AND THE DELIGHT OF THE AUDIENCE

When we speak poetry we sometimes concentrate on the wrong things. Let's continue to use *Verse* as the illustration. In speaking this, we are not concerned with making beautiful or musical sounds as if we were some kind of vocalist, nor are we saying this poem in order to impose some kind of 'explanation' or gloss on it. Our intention must be to convey wholly the intention Landor had in mind when writing the piece. The speaker is the mouthpiece (or, to vary the metaphor, the servant) of the poet. In speaking, the meaning must be made clear and we use the technical proficiency at our command to do this but without in any way calling attention to our efforts. One has to realise that meaning and form are inextricably linked: that is why I couldn't tell you in a purely factual way what *Verse* meant. The form of the poem has to be given to the listener together with the meaning, which is why one must be aware of the pattern of the poem, the pattern of the lines, the rhymes and the rhythm as well as the other devices Landor uses. One must be aware, too, of the atmosphere Landor creates: in the first stanza this is one of joy which changes in the second to languid sadness. The tone of the poem and the diction must be noted. Here the words are simple and direct and yet they convey the atmosphere. The depth of the contrasting emotions of joy and sadness as change and death occur tells us about the pace of the piece and so do such prosaic details as the length of the vowels running through a line. It is only when one has become the messenger of Walter Savage

Landor that the listener, almost unconsciously until he thinks afterwards about his response to the speaking, is able to say, 'I have experienced something sublime'. It is for this reason that you work at relaxation and precision and flexibility in speaking; it is for this reason, too, that you extend the range of your voice and build up the ability to express a whole rainbow of emotions: simply that you may be a good servant of the poet.

SOME NOTES ON VERSE MEASURES

When we looked at the metrical pattern in *Verse* we noted that there were four iambic feet to the line (iambic tetrameters). A poem may be written in measures other than the iambic. There are also the trochaic, anapaestic and dactylic. You will find yourself dealing more securely with the speaking of your selected poem if you are able to understand its metre and rhythm.

TROCHAIC MEASURE

Generally there are either three or four trochaic feet to the line. Three strong beats to the line create a simple but satisfying rhythm of:

/STRONG weak/ STRONG weak/ STRONG weak/

as the first verse of Sabine Baring Gould's well-known hymn shows:

> Now the day is over,
> Night is drawing nigh;
> Shadows of the evening
> Steal across the sky.

The second and fourth lines maintain the three strong beats but the final weak syllable in each case is missing.

Trochaic measure with four strong beats to the line:

/STRONG weak/ STRONG weak/ STRONG weak/ STRONG weak/)

can be found in Longfellow's lengthy poem *Hiawatha* and in many of Tennyson's and Shelley's poems. As an example, here are the first four lines of Edward Osler's hymn in the Foundling Hospital Collection:

> Praise the Lord! ye heavens, adore him;
> Praise him, angels, in the height;
> Sun and moon, rejoice before him,
> Praise him, all ye stars and light

Note, again, the absence of a weak syllable at the ends of lines two and four.

ANAPAESTIC MEASURE

The anapaestic and the dactylic measures are used less frequently than the iambic and trochaic. The anapaestic measure consists of two weak syllables and a strong beat: it can be heard in words such as 'dis-ap-PEAR' and 'in-ter-RUPT'. Lord Byron wrote *The Destruction of Sennacherib* in this measure of which the first verse runs:

> The Assyrian came down like the wolf on the fold,
> And his cohorts were gleaming in purple and gold;
> And the sheen of their spears was like stars on the sea,
> When the blue wave rolls nightly on deep Galilee.

From this you notice that the rhythm gives a fine propelling motion to the verse.

DACTYLIC MEASURE

A dactyl consists of a strong beat followed by two weak syllables. Poets often find two feet to a line workable as this verse from *The Charge of the Light Brigade,* by Alfred, Lord Tennyson shows:

> Cannon to right of them,
> Cannon to left of them,
> Cannon in front of them,
> Volleyed and thundered.
> Stormed at with shot and shell,
> Boldly they rode and well,

> Into the jaws of death,
> Into the mouth of hell,
> Rode the six hundred.

It is possible to double the length of the line (/STRONG weak weak/ STRONG weak weak/ STRONG weak weak/ STRONG weak weak/) as 'G D' does in his *Railway Dactyls* in which the sound of the train's wheels passing over the rails is suggested:

> Here we go off on the 'London and Birmingham',
> Bidding adieu to the foggy metropolis!
> Staying at home with the dumps in confirming 'em:
> Motion and mirth are a fillip to life.

THE SPONDEE

One foot remains to mention. This is the spondee, consisting of two strong beats. It is sometimes used by poets at the end of a line – although it may be otherwise placed – instead of an iamb or a trochee. In this iambic line Pope replaces the last foot with a spondee:

> Yet tames not this, it sticks to our last sand.

RESOURCES

Books on Poetry

Blackburn, T (ed), *Presenting Poetry* (1966)
Brewer, R F, *The Art of Versification and the Techniques of Poetry* (1962)
Fraser G S, *Metre, Rhyme and Free Verse* (1970)
Hughes, T, *Poetry in the Making* (1967)
Reeves, J, *Understanding Poetry* (1979)
Roberts, P, *How Poetry Works* (1986)
Spender, S, *The Making of a Poem* (1955)

Books on verse speaking

Crump, G, *Speaking Poetry* (1964)
Mulcahy, B, *How to Speak a Poem* (1988)
Mulcahy, B, *To Speak True* (1969)

There is a useful chapter on verse speaking in *Voice and Speech* (1939) by Gwynneth L Thurburn.

Poetry anthologies

Adcock, Fleur, ed, *The Faber Book of Twentieth Century Women's Poetry* (1987)

Amis, Kingsley, ed, *The Faber Popular Reciter* (1978)

Applefield, David, et al, eds, *Five Readings* (1991)

Baker, Kenneth, ed, *The Faber Book of English History in Verse* (1988)

Cosman, Carol, et al, eds, *The Penguin Book of Women Poets* (1978)

Dunn, Sara, ed, *Beneath the Wide, Wide Heaven* (1991) (poems on the environment)

Feinstein, Elaine, ed, *New Poetry II* (1988)

Field, Jonathan and Moira, eds, *The Methuen Book of Theatre Verse* (1991)

Foster, John, ed, *Let's Celebrate. Festival Poems* (1989) (designed for schools but contains adult material)

Gardner, Brian, ed, *The Terrible Rain, The War Poets* 1939 – 1945 (1981)

Gardner, Helen, ed, *The New Oxford Book of English Verse* (1972)

Hunt, John Dixon, ed, *The Oxford Book of Garden Verse* (1993)

Kinsella, Thomas, ed, *The New Oxford Book of Irish Verse* (1968)

Lonsdale, Roger, ed, *Eighteenth Century Women Poets* (1989)

Lucie-Smith, Edward, ed, *British Poetry since 1945* (1970)

MacMonagle, Niall, ed, *Lifelines. An Anthology of Poems Chosen by Famous People* (1985)

McGann, Jerome, ed, *The Oxford Book of Romantic Period Verse* (1993)

Nye, Robert, ed *New Poetry I* (nd)

Olden, David, ed, *Seven Ages. Poetry for a Lifetime* (1992)

Ormsby, Frank, ed, *Rage for Order. Poetry of the Northern Ireland Troubles* (1992)

Osborne, Charles, ed, *The Collins Book of Best Loved Verse* (1986)

Roberts, Susan, ed, *Poetry Please* (1991)

Rosen, Michael, ed, *The Kingfisher Book of Children's Poetry* (1985) (contains much material for adults)

Scammell, William, ed, *This Green Earth. A Celebration of Nature Poetry* (1992)

Sieghart, William, ed, *The Forward Book of Poetry* (1992)

Stallworthy, Jon, ed, *The Penguin Book of Love Poetry* (1973)

Wain, John, ed, *The Oxford Anthology of English Poetry. Blake to Heaney* (1986)

Audio tapes

There is much about poetry selection and speaking in *Speak the Speech*, a set of audio tapes devised and presented by Dr Kenneth Pickering and available from Pinner Sound, 47 High Street, Pinner, Middlesex HA5 5PJ.

3

THE SONNET

When we look at the form or structure of a sonnet we can expect to find the following features:

- invariably the sonnet consists of fourteen lines. These are usually organised in a group of eight lines, the octave, followed by a group of six, the sestet. The way in which these two blocks are used by poets to develop their material varies

- the rhyming scheme also varies according to the type of sonnet and is discussed below

- the metrical pattern is composed of iambic pentameters. Inversions and the substitution of spondees occur

There are historical and literary reasons for the various forms of the sonnet. Those discussed in the sections below are the most common.

THE PETRARCHAN OR ITALIAN SONNET

Key work: *Upon Westminster Bridge* by William Wordsworth

The sonnet form is of Italian origin dating back to the Renaissance and was used by both Petrarch and Dante. The Petrarchan Sonnet consists of:

- fourteen lines divided into octave and sestet

- the octave is made up of two quatrains (a quatrain is a set of four lines)

- the sestet is composed of two tercets (or sets of three lines)

- when the sonnet is written in Italian the rhyming scheme is limited. In the octave only two rhymes are the norm: *abba abba*

- three pairs of rhymes are usually found in the tercet: *cde cde*

The subject consists of one idea which is stated, often in universal terms, boldly in the first quatrain and developed in the second. A pause then follows. In each of the two tercets the subject is again considered but this time it tends to be particularised. Finally it is brought to a definite and forceful close. This fascinating mix of compression and elaboration is to be found in the various forms of the poem.

The Petrarchan Sonnet was introduced from Italy into England by Sir Thomas Wyatt and developed by Henry Howard, Earl of Surrey. Difficulties were encountered. Italian is a musical and flexible language, far more so than English, and in order to accommodate the language change extra rhymes had to be incorporated. A second change in the form was the rearrangement of the sestet in a variety of ways: sometimes the change would be in the rhyming scheme which was altered to *cd cd cd* with the sense contained in the series of three couplets (a set of two lines) instead of spread over two tercets. In England the form became more flexible than in Italy.

As an example of the English development of the Petrarchan Sonnet let us look at William Wordsworth's poem *Upon Westminster Bridge*.

Earth has not anything to show more fair:
Dull would he be of soul who could pass by
A sight so touching in its majesty:
This city now doth, like a garment, wear
The beauty of the morning; silent, bare,
Ships, towers, domes, theatres, and temples lie
Open unto the fields, and to the sky:
All bright and glittering in the smokeless air.
Never did sun more beautifully steep

> In his first splendour, valley, rock, or hill;
> Ne'er saw I, never felt, a calm so deep!
> The river glideth at his own sweet will:
> Dear God! the very houses seem asleep;
> And all that mighty heart is lying still.

Although Wordsworth lived for much of his life in sparsely populated areas, he had a great love of the crowds and bustle of London. The townscape of the poem is almost deserted but the writer is conscious of the many people living in the city. On 31 July 1802 Wordsworth and his sister Dorothy took the coach to Dover on their way to France and crossed Westminster Bridge early in the morning. Dorothy described the scene in her notebook:

> The city, St Paul's, with the river and a multitude of little boats made a most beautiful sight...The houses were not overhung by their cloud of smoke, and they were spread out endlessly, yet the sun shone so brightly, with such a fierce light, that there was even something like the purity of one of nature's own grand spectacles.

William, as much as his sister, was awed by the early morning changes of light as his poem, written at the beginning of the following September, reveals.

Magnificently Wordsworth marries form and meaning. In his hands the sonnet form becomes malleable, like clay, and the poet can shape it to serve his purpose. There are two full stops in the poem marking the end of the octave and the sestet. Although Wordsworth gives us the conventional rhymes of the octave *abba abba*, yet he transcends this scheme in his description. The first three lines are a trumpet blast of a statement, – but he keeps us guessing what the subject is really going to be. From the fourth line to the end of the octave he describes the City of Westminster, then so compact that the surrounding fields could still be seen. The last line of the octave is a summary of the description and, in spite of the preceding colon, it must issue from the word painting and not be treated as a separate sentence. In the sestet the meaning again breaks away from the traditional confines of the form. The description continues for another four lines and then with 'Dear God!' the mood and meaning change. Half in prayer and half in awe Wordsworth contemplates the silence of the city in the early morning. The last line is much more than a description: it is a philosophical statement about the unity of mankind in the city and the chosen vocabulary recalls the title of St Augustine's work *The City of God* in which the bishop sees the world and the church as a great urban society under the sovereignty of God.

In your speaking you need to convey this progression of ideas expressed within the form Wordsworth has chosen. The great statement of the poem is in the last line; paradoxically it cannot be spoken loudly or forcefully. As I've mentioned, silence is one of the qualities of this poem and an exceptionally difficult one to convey in speaking. The final line of the octave must also summarise the description of early-morning Westminster, but this line is of lesser importance than the final.

You need also to take note of the metrical form. We expect it to be a series of iambic pentameters and indeed it is. However, the iambic foot is often reversed. The first occasion is at the opening of the sonnet:

EARTH has not ANything to SHOW more FAIR

The effect of the substitution of a trochee at the beginning of the second line is to push the verse forward and you can hear this if you read the words aloud:

DULL would he BE...

The last foot of line 12 is a spondee (two strong beats):

The river glideth at his own SWEET WILL

which indicates a slight prolongation of the words, letting the sound mirror the sense and picture. But when we arrive at the last line the regularity of the metre is almost an imitation of the corporate heartbeat of the city:

And ALL that MIGHTy HEART is LYing STILL!

By now you will have noticed that in the octave lines 2, 4 and 6 are without terminal punctuation; it should be said again that it is most important to maintain the flow of the sense without reducing the linear rhythm to continuous prose. This challenge has been dealt with in the previous chapter. The kind of listings Wordsworth uses necessitates peppering some lines with commas: lines 6 and 10 are examples. Try to convey the whole line rather than the individual words within it; to this end make the pauses at the commas inserted between words fractional so that they barely exist. The semi-colon in line 5 poses a different problem. Here there is a termination of sense but in the last three syllables is the beginning of a new description. Your voice must therefore do three things effortlessly: there is a partial conclusion to suggest, a new description to begin and the rhythm of the line to maintain. This is difficult to achieve and success with this is a mark of your skill as a verse speaker.

I've heard this poem many times. Often the lasting impression is that it has been spoken too quickly. Wordsworth is in a quiet, contemplative mood and that recollection of the scene and the awe expressed at the poem's end must be given just measure.

Anthologies

William Wordsworth, *Selected Poetry and Prose*, ed Philip Hobsbaum (1989)
William Wordsworth, *Selected Poetry*, ed Nicholas Roe (1992)

Background reading

Gill, Stephen, *William Wordsworth* (1989)
Noyes, Russell, *Wordsworth and the Art of Landscape* (1968)

THE SHAKESPEAREAN SONNET

Key work: *Sonnet 29* by William Shakespeare

William Shakespeare developed the sonnet form. The Shakespearean sonnet departs from the tightly interlaced model of the Petrarchan and in its place a form is used which, although it still consists of an octave and a sestet with a pause between the two, breaks these into different shapes:

- the octave is divided into two quatrains, made distinct by the rhyme scheme which runs: *abab cdcd*
- the sestet consists of a quatrain, *efef*
- and a final couplet, *gg*

This pattern allows Shakespeare:

- to present an argument in the octave
- to recognise either a development or a contradiction of this in the first four lines of the sestet
- to make a strong concluding statement in the couplet

Let us see how this works out in practice using as an example *Sonnet 29*.

> When, in disgrace with Fortune and men's eyes,
> I all alone beweep my outcast state,
> And trouble deaf heaven with my bootless cries,
> And look upon myself and curse my fate,
> Wishing me like to one more rich in hope,
> Featured like him, like him with friends possessed,
> Desiring this man's art, and that man's scope,
> With what I most enjoy contented least;
> Yet in these thoughts myself almost despising,
> Haply I think on thee, and then my state,
> Like to the lark at break of day arising
> From sullen earth, sings hymns at heaven's gate;
> For thy sweet love rememb'red such wealth brings,
> That then I scorn to change my state with kings.

Unlike Wordsworth in the previous sonnet, Shakespeare isn't writing a description; his subject is more complex. This is one of a group of sonnets Shakespeare addressed to 'the Friend', possibly his patron, the wealthy, young Earl of Southampton with whom, some say, Shakespeare was in love. Who is the 'I' of the sonnet? Many would opt for Shakespeare himself but this is not a necessity and many more recent poets use an 'I' which is fictional. Assuming that here Shakespeare is speaking, we have a picture of an actor-playwright losing his contentment with the world of the theatre and wishing that he had instead been born into the more expansive world of the nobility. But this leads him to think of his patron and instantly the thought fills him with joy and fulfilment. So this poem is the record of one man's journey from despair to the dawning of happiness. In his image of the rising lark Shakespeare conveys with artistry the man's rise in spirits.

How do these ideas fit the form? The octave begins with the word 'When' and this word governs the next eight lines until the speaker arrives at the 'Yet' at the beginning of the sestet which heralds a change of mood. It is not a sudden change: the writer gradually introduces the notion of sweet contentment. The whole poem is a contrast between two states, that of the work-a-day actor and that of the wealthy aristocrat; the contrast of discontent with happiness in one's lot. There is even a contrast in the resolution of the last couplet: Shakespeare refuses to change his lowly status with that of a king.

How do these considerations affect the speaking of the poem? Firstly consider who you are speaking to and then go on to think about the relationship of the person addressed and the speaker; this will help to establish the vocal tone. The speaker is making a journey from despair (the first eight lines) through to joy (lines 9 to 12) which is ultimately summed up in a two line statement – almost a resolution (lines 13 and 14). The word 'When' governs the octave and you need to keep the drive of the poem going until you reach the end of line 8. Similarly that word 'Yet' must then see the poem through to the conclusion. Possibly you have observed that at the beginning of each section a reversal of the opening iamb occurs:

WHEN in disGRACE...

and

YET in these THOUGHTS...

These reversals help to maintain both drive and pace. Much of the emotional drive of the poem comes in the vowel sounds, so give these their true value and maintain projection to the end of each line in order to maintain strength of speech.

An accomplished performer would be able to speak the octave on one breath and the sestet on another. But for your own purposes the breath must be made rapidly and silently at the end-of-line punctuation points. Line 11 is in the nature of a parenthesis and sometimes is printed in brackets: you may deal with this by dropping the pitch of your voice slightly on this line alone and also by increasing the pace, but do this with subtlety.

A sonnet is a formal statement and so there must be a degree of formality in your physical appearance, seen in both your clothes and your posture: either sitting or standing would be appropriate but whichever, be careful to maintain a conscious dignity.

An edition of William Shakespeare's sonnets

Shakespeare, William, *The Sonnets*, ed William Burton (1964)

Books on William Shakespeare's sonnets

Bloom, Harold, *Shakespeare's Sonnets* (1987)
Vendler, Helen, *The Ways into Shakespeare's Sonnets* (1990)
Wait, R J C, *The Background to Shakespeare's Sonnets* (1972)

EXAMPLES OF SONNETS

Some sequences of sonnets

C Day Lewis: *O Dreams! O Destinations!*
William Shakespeare: *Sonnets*
Philip Sidney: *Astrophel and Stella*
Edmund Spenser: *Amoretti*

A dozen individual sonnets

W H Auden: *Who's Who*
George Barker: *Sonnet to my Mother*
Rupert Brooke: *The Soldier*
Roy Campbell: *The Zebras*
John Donne: *Batter my heart, three person'd God*
John Keats: *On first looking into Chapman's Homer*
Wilfred Owen: *Anthem to Doomed Youth*
Alexander Pope: *Mrs Reynold's Cat*
Christina Rosetti: *Remember*
P B Shelley: *Ozymandias*
Dylan Thomas: *When all my Five and Country Senses See*
William Wordsworth: *The World is too much with Us*

General works on the sonnet

Crutwell, B, *The English Sonnet* (1966)
Fuller, J, *The Sonnet* (1972)
Lever, J W, *The Elizabethan Love Sonnet* (1968)
Nye, R, *A Book of Sonnets* (1976)
Spiller, M R G, *The Development of the Sonnet: an Introduction* (1992)

4

LYRICAL VERSE

We can see at once that 'lyrical' has some affinity with the word 'lyre'. This is a stringed instrument, resembling a small harp, which originally was used as a background to spoken or chanted poetry. Lyrical verse still maintains this link, for it is quiet and reflective and has a musical quality. Another characteristic is that it expresses the individual emotions of the poet. These two qualities are a guide to the performer: in speaking lyric verse we are working on a small scale so the speaking is intimate, musical, thoughtful and personal. There is no set form for lyric verse.

I have chosen three key works to illustrate this chapter. The first is by a contemporary poet, John Walsh, *The Christmas Tree*, selected for its simplicity. Don't be misled, for poetic simplicity is very difficult to come to terms with. The second poem is *Duns Scotus's Oxford* by Gerard Manley Hopkins; this allows me to write briefly about sprung rhythm, not necessarily a characteristic of lyrical verse, but a rhythm favoured by Hopkins. A metaphysical poem by John Donne, *The Sunne Rising*, serves as an introduction to poetry which is highly intellectual and overbrimming with wit, using the language of direct speech.

Key work: *The Christmas Tree* by John Walsh

> They chopped her down in some far wood
> A week ago.
> Shook from her dark green spikes her load
> Of gathered snow.
> And brought her home at last, to be
> Our Christmas show.
>
> A week she shone, sprinkled with lamps
> And fairy frost;

> Now, with her boughs all stripped, her lights
> And spangles lost.
> Out in the garden there, leaning
> On a broken post.
>
> She sighs gently...Can it be
> She longs to go
> Back to that far-off wood, where green
> And wild things grow?
> Back to her dark green sisters, standing
> In wind and snow.

Sometimes I have heard the first two lines spoken:

> They chopped her down in some far wood a week ago.

What has happened? The pattern of the poetry has been rearranged, resulting in a change of emphasis and, surprisingly, meaning. Try saying the line as it is printed above and then as given in the complete poem. When 'A week ago' stands as a single line, attention is drawn to the time scale which is going to be adopted in the poem and to which reference is made a number of times: it is the passing from the beauty of stanza 1 to the exoticism of the second and the longing (and maybe rejection) of the final stanza. Something similar happens in the last line of the first stanza: there is great pride in the simple statement that the tree is the king post of the Christmas show and the slight suspensory pause at the end of the previous line serves to emphasize this. In the final question, at the end of the poem, the brief line 'In wind and snow?' again gives us an emphasis: the place of wildness and weather is the true home of the fir tree. The pattern of the poetry is important.

Have you noticed that the rhyme sound of the first stanza (ago, snow, show) is used again in the final one (go, grow, snow) and that this gives a feeling of completion? The rhymes in the second stanza are used to effect also. The word 'frost' comes at the end of a couplet telling of the colourful days of the tree and 'lost' at the end of a description of the stripped tree. But just as we are expecting a rhyme of similar sound, Walsh uses an eye rhyme ('post' looks as though it rhymes with 'frost' and 'lost' but the sound is different) which draws our attention to the hapless tree, seemingly sharing the same fate as the broken post. Rhymes can have a strange psychological effect on the listener.

The metre is important but treat it lightly and create a pleasant contrast between the line lengths. In these, lines of four iambic feet alternate with lines of two feet. The last stanza contains a line of three dots. These represent one of the weak syllables in the line and you must allow time for the missing sound: cleverly this use of rhythm helps to reinforce through silence the gently made sigh of the tree.

Although the poem looks so simple to speak, even after a cursorary glance you realise that it raises a number of challenges for the speaker.

Key work: *Duns Scotus's Oxford* by Gerard Manley Hopkins

Gerard Manley Hopkins was a Jesuit priest whose poetry was written in the 1860s and thereafter. The first job is to read the text of *Duns Scotus's Oxford* carefully and set the names and allusions in some kind of context:

Towery city and branchy between towers;
Cuckoo-echoing, bell-swarmed, lark-charmed,
    rook-racked, river-rounded;
The dapple-eared lily below thee; that country and
    town did
Once encounter in, here coped and poised powers.

Thou hast a base and brickish skirt there, sours
That neighbour-nature thy grey beauty is grounded
Best in; graceless growth, thou hast confounded
Rural rural-keeping – folk, flocks, and flowers.

Yet ah! this air I gather and I release
He lived on; these weeds and waters, these walls are what
He haunted who of all men most sways my spirits to peace;

Of realty the rarest-veined unraveller; a not
Rivalled insight, be rival Italy or Greece;
Who fired France for Mary without spot.

Duns Scotus (c1265-1308) was a Franciscan friar and philosopher, the first great theologian to defend the doctrine of the Immaculate Conception of Mary (that Mary was, unlike the rest of humanity, born without original sin), which is the substance of the final line of the poem. Scotus was said to have worked in Oxford for the last few years of his short life. One can sum up his teaching by saying that Scotus saw the material world not as matter divorced from God but as a symbol of God. Thus there was, for him, a holiness in the everyday.

In 1879, when he wrote this poem, Hopkins was one of the curates of St Aloysius's Church, Oxford, and before starting the sonnet he had read one set of the works of Scotus (a commentary on the writings of Peter Lombard, in turn a twelfth-century theologian) with tremendous enthusiasm: here was a kindred spirit.

The first stanza of the poem is a magnificent description of Oxford as it existed in the fourteenth century, a place of towers and trees surrounded by the river Thames, all integrated with the surrounding countryside. Unfortunately by the nineteenth century, when Hopkins was writing, the 'base and brickish skirt' – the Victorian brick terraces – detracted from the beauty of the medieval city. One of Hopkins' diary entries refers to Oxford as 'abridged and soured'. By the third verse Hopkins is thinking of Duns Scotus, a real presence in Oxford, enjoying the same air and sights as the poet. The final stanza refers to the writings of Scotus on the exact nature of the individual (this is why the philosopher is, for Hopkins, 'the unraveller') and this theme is picked up in the reference to Mary. Her name comes into the piece unexpectedly unless you are aware of Hopkins' background thoughts in introducing the first word of the poem, 'Towery'. He has in mind some of the poetic references that are made to Mary in the Litany of Loreto in which she is referred to as 'Tower of Ivory', 'Tower of David'.

So the poem begins with Mary as well as ending with a thought of her. The final line means: It was France, not Oxford, which was fired by the teaching of Duns Scotus about the sinlessness of Mary.

The poem is written in sonnet form: the first half concerns Oxford and the second the unnamed philosopher. The limited rhyming scheme helps to bind the poem together, in the first two stanzas running *abba abba*, and in stanzas three and four, *cdc dcd*. However, the complexity of the writing is in the rhythm which Hopkins described as 'sprung'. In order to speak the poem successfully one needs to come to terms with the mechanics of this.

Hopkins explained his rhythmic scheme in a letter he wrote to the Revd R W Dixon. His argument was that a line would have a predetermined number of stresses and an undetermined number of weak syllables. In most writing there is a predetermined number of both unstressed and stressed syllables. As with a conventional sonnet written in iambic pentameters, there are five stresses in each line of *Duns Scotus's Oxford*. This may be heard clearly in the first:

TOWERy CIty and BRANCHy beTWEEN TOWers

The length of the next line illustrates Hopkins' premise that there may be any number of unstressed syllables:

CUCKoo-echoing, BELL-swarmed, LARK-charmed, ROOK-racked, river-ROUNDed

The decision to use any number of unstressed syllables allowed the poet much greater freedom than a conventional metrical scheme would because the lines are for the benefit of the listener's ear and not the reader's eye. When you prepare the poem for speaking you must discover the stresses and feel them, almost unconsciously, repeated through each line.

The second line of the poem also introduces Hopkins' delight in taking two common words and creating a compound by hyphenating them together. A poetry speaker must be aware that he is to give the time value of a single spoken word to the compound, without, of course, resorting to a mechanical approach; the result is that the poetry seems to gain in momentum with the hyphenations. Flexibility is seen in the transference of the stressed syllable at the end of the line. My own reckoning, not Hopkins', is that the first four stresses occur on the complete noun or part of it as a long vowel is generally a stressed syllable. On arriving at the last of the compounds, 'river' is made up of a short 'i' sound followed by the neutral vowel (a lightly made 'er' sound) and the natural tendency is to place the stress on the first syllable of 'rounded' in which the 'ow' vowel is indeed long. This creates a reversal: the stress is not in the expected place but gives way to unstressed syllables with the effect that the line is 'counterpointed', Hopkins' term for the strong syncopation which can be heard. It is usually sufficient to be aware of these rhythmic changes and to allow your speaking to reflect them without drawing the attention of the listener to them.

Other devices elaborate the sound texture. There is alliteration (repetitions of a consonant) such as the recurring 'r' in 'rook-racked, river-rounded' and later the cluster 'folk, flocks and flowers'. Hopkins moves beyond initial letters: 'dapple-eared' has a repeated 'd' at both the start and ending of the compound and spread richly throughout the last stanza are the recurring 'r' and 'v' consonants. The speaker may easily over-articulate these in a misplaced attempt to force the music of the poem which would be wrong, for whilst he must be aware of the devices Hopkins is employing, the aim is to convey the poet's message, in the poet's own way, to the listener. Over-articulation would be a distraction.

Assonance (the repeated use of the same vowel) can create a similar complexity of sound. In the penultimate line a long 'i' sound is contained within 'rival', 'rivalled' and 'insight'. This may be compared with the changing mouth positions and consequent varying pronunciations of the 'a' sounds in 'yet ah! this air I gather'. The exhalation on 'ah' symbolises the passing air which Hopkins mentions.

Sometimes a sound occuring at the beginning and end of a line binds that sub-section of the poem together:

thOU hast a base and brickish skirt there, sOUrs

At other times a vowel is repeated, engaging in this instance a word which could well be made redundant on its second appearance: 'I gather and I release'.

Lastly there is the imagery. In establishing the vista of the medieval city, images consist of towers, interspersing tree branches, the river and birds, later summarised under the selected icons of 'these weeds and waters, these walls'. Red-brick building, especially in the district known as Jericho, a grid of streets housing the workers of the University Press, is summed up in the unusual metaphor of the skirt in stanza two; then, with such speed that it is almost a mixed metaphor, the notion of a soured countryside, spoilt like soured milk, is broached. Hopkins goes on to speak of Scotus. For him, he is 'Of realty the rarest-veined unraveller' and one wonders why exactly that adjective is used of the philosopher: does the compound suggest bloodlessness or unworldliness? Many such questions could be asked but they would probably remain unanswered. Notice the antithesis (placing strong contrasts side by side) in the idea of Scotus as the one who haunts – a metaphor of a ghostly activity – bringing peace to the poet's spirits, again a supernatural word.

This, then, is a complex poem, strange in both its message and presentation. The speaker has to unravel the complicated text for the listener: to do that he must make the poem his own through study and practice.

Anthology

Hopkins, Gerard Manley, *Poems and Prose*, ed W H Gardner (1953)

Books on Gerard Manley Hopkins

Gardner, W H, *Gerard Manley Hopkins (1846 – 1889). A Study of Poetic Idiosyncracy in Relation to Poetic Tradition* (1944)

Mackenzie, Norman H, *A Reader's Guide to Gerard Manley Hopkins* (1981)

Martin, R B, *Gerard Manley Hopkins: a very private life*(1991)

White, Norman, *Hopkins, a Literary Biography* (1992)

Key work: *The Sunne Rising* by John Donne

The sixteenth and seventeenth-century writer, John Donne, was an adventurer, poet and clergyman, rising ultimately to the eminent position of Dean of St Paul's Cathedral in London. His religious, or 'divine', poems illustrate his firm personal belief, and in contrast his love poems reveal a passionate voluptuary. If you are reading this poem for the first time you will realise that the 'voice' of Donne is that of a poet who uses the idiomatic speech of his day. It is direct, impatient and, above all, impassioned.

> Busie old foole, unruly Sunne,
> Why dost thou thus,
> Through windowes, and through curtains call on us?
> Must to thy motions lovers seasons run?
> Sawcy pedantique wretch, goe chide
> Late schoole boyes and sowre prentices,
> Goe tell Court-huntsmen, that the King will ride,
> Call country ants to harvest offices;
> Love, all alike, no season knowes, nor clyme,
> Nor houres, dayes, moneths, which are the rags of time.
>
> Thy beames, so reverend, and strong
> Why shouldst thou thinke?
> I could eclipse and cloud them with a winke,
> But that I would not lose her sight so long:
> If her eyes have not blinded thine,
> Looke, and tomorrow late, tell mee,
> Whether both th 'India's of spice and Myne
> Be where thou leftest them, or lie here with mee.
> Ask for those Kings whom thou saw'st yesterday,
> And thou shalt heare, All here in one bed lay.
>
> She'is all States, and all Princes, I,
> Nothing else is.

Princes do but play us; compar'd to this,
All honor's mimique; all wealth alchimie.
      Thou sunne art halfe as happy'as wee,
       In that the world's contracted thus;
    Thine age askes ease, and since thy duties bee
    To warme the world, that's done in warming us.
Shine here to us, and thou art every where;
This bed thy center is, these walls, thy sphere.

Donne is lying in bed, not with his wife but with an imagined mistress, as the sun begins to rise. The poet adopts a scathing, imperious tone when addressing the sun but at the same time there is a reflection of the deep passion he feels for his fictitious mistress, a feeling probably based on that for his wife Ann. The sheer complicatedness of the ideas inherent in the piece demand that the work is spoken in a measured way, that they may be discerned and savoured. Added to this is the intensity of the passion which also precludes hurry: 'To read Donne you must measure Time and discover the time of each word by the sense of passion,' wrote Edith Sitwell. That remark truly applies to *The Sunne Rising.*

The first step is to come to terms with the contemporary ideas expressed. There is a movement away from the 'singing note' of earlier poets. Instead Donne addresses the sun as an old fool, a teacher or a lackey who will contact schoolboys, apprentices and the huntsmen of the royal court of James I, a great devotee not only of hunting but of all physical activities. He ends the stanza with the affirmation that love exists beyond the rule of times and seasons.

The second stanza centres on an image Donne often uses, that of eyes. He asks why the sun imagines that his beams are strong when Donne can make them disappear by shutting his eyes, except that he is unwilling to lose the sight of his mistress. In the second half a physical reality is reversed: the eyes of the mistress could dazzle the sun. He then, both in this and the next verse, pictures the sun making its way round the world on a system of concentric spheres (so the Alexandrian mathematician, Ptolemy, explained in the second century before the birth of Christ the movement of the sun and planets) and asks him to check whether the spices of the orient or the rulers of the various kingdoms are still at home or joined with him and his mistress: for Donne his mistress has become the centre of all things, a conceit (or witty idea) which he extends into stanza 3.

His device of using the obverse of a truth (for instance, that the rays from human eyes can blind the eyes of the sun) is again put to use. Princes, he claims, imitate the lover and his mistress; honour is merely an empty show and wealth is simply the chemical change of dross to gold. The contrast of appearance and reality is stressed in Donne's use of the word 'play' in 'Princes do but play us': princes are demoted to actors playing a role. He also returns to the idea that he and his mistress are a microcosm of the world and if the sun's business is to warm the world, then that is done in warming the two lovers.

How does this intellectual grasp of the text help in speaking the poem? Firstly, it must be spoken with understanding. You must not only know in general the meaning of the piece – something which too many candidates rest content with – but you must also be aware why Donne chose his key words.

Secondly, you must be aware of the tone of the poem. In the first four lines this is set: a man is hurling abuse at the sun. But there are counteracting tones, too, to bring out, foremost the passionate love of the writer. There are also the ideas of the period (the importance of geographic discovery, changing theories on alchemy and astronomy, the political role of the prince in the state) which alert us to the fact that here is no sequestered romantic but a man who is alive to progress and change. This factor introduces another dimension in the speaking: the 'I' (a pronoun which in this poem needs stressing) of the poem is a thrusting intellectual.

Take heed of the punctuation. This will help you to discover the 'voice' of the poet. Mark the line as well as the way in which Donne suggests that you sort out the meaning within it. The voice of the poet is expressed in the line pattern and it would be inappropriate to allow commas to chop into the line lengths.

With Donne, and indeed with any of the other metaphysical poets who deal with passion and ideas through contrasting and sometimes disparate images, you need to read a quantity of the writer's output. That way you become at home with his expression and this will help you to avoid a preciousness which will grate and give the lie to the poet's message. I would suggest the following give an interesting insight into Donne's ways of thought and expression: *A Valediction: Forbidding Mourning*, *The Relique*, *The Good-Morrow*, *A Hymne to God the Father* and the *Hymne to God my God, in my Sicknesse*.

Anthologies

John Hayward has arranged and introduced a selection of the poetry of Donne in *John Donne. A Selection of His Poetry* (1950). He also appears, this time in context, with introductory and biographical notes by Helen Gardner in *The Metaphysical Poets* (1957).

Books on John Donne

Carey, John, *John Donne, His Life, Mind and Art* (1981)
Parfitt, George, *John Donne – A Literary Life* (1989)
Smith, A J, *John Donne: the Songs and Sonnets* (1964)
Winny, James, *A Preface to Donne* (1970)

OTHER TYPES OF LYRIC VERSE
The Ode

Almost any kind of song would, by definition, fit into the category of lyric verse and the word 'ode' stems from the Greek word meaning 'to sing'. Odes were a feature of the Greek drama of the fifth century BC. Each tragedy usually contained five episodes in which the action took place; between these the chorus would offer a commentary in the form of odes on the activity the audience had witnessed. These were performed by the chorus dividing into two sections; one section sang the strophe, possibly whilst the other half of the chorus danced and in reply the antistrophe, verses identical in shape with those of the strophe, was sung by the previously silent half; finally the epode were sung in unison. The odes in the *Oresteia* by Aeschylus and in the *Theban Trilogy* of Sophocles are justly famed. *Athens* by Algernon Swinburne is one of the few odes in English to preserve the Greek classical model.

The Greek Ode:
Plays

Aeschylus, *The Oresteian Trilogy*, trans Philip Vellacott (1956)

Sophocles, *Three Theban Plays*, trans Robert Fagles (1984)

Books on Greek Theatre and the Greek Chorus

Arnott, P D, *An Introduction to the Greek Theatre* (1959)

Baldry, H C, *The Greek Tragic Theatre* (1978)

Simon, Erica, trans Vafopoulou-Richardson, C E, *The Ancient Theatre* (1982)

The Romantic Ode: John Keats

In the course of time an ode became addressed to a particular person or object: John Keats wrote an *Ode to a Nightingale* after sitting in his garden at Hampstead listening to this bird singing. In the poem he meditated on the immortal beauty of the bird's song and the sorrow of the listener as he realised that all things were changing and passing away. Another of Keats' odes was prompted by a Grecian urn: looking at the imagined pastoral scenes on this, Keats reflected on the eternal quality of art and the transitoriness of human happiness. *To Autumn* has the characteristics of an ode: autumn is lightly personified as a figure in a variety of autumnal landscapes, the latter suggested by the water meadows at Winchester, and the passing of summer is seen as a parallel with the transience of life.

Collected Poetry

Keats, John, *The Complete Poems*, ed John Barnard (1973)

The Romantic Ode: Percy Bysshe Shelley

Another of the Romantics, Percy Bysshe Shelley, wrote a number of odes. *To a Skylark* is a song in praise of freedom and *The Ode to the West Wind* is a series of five sonnet-like stanzas revealing Shelley's minute observation of wind, water, wood, cloud and sky: in the poem hope and energy are achieved through suffering and despair.

Anthology

Shelley, P B, *Selected Poetry*, ed Isabel Quigly (1956)

Works on Shelley

Holmes, Richard, *Shelley – The Pursuit* (1974)
Tomalin, Claire, *Shelley and his World* (1984)

A selection of odes by other writers

John Milton: *L'Allegro, Il Penseroso, Lycidas*
John Dryden: *Alexander's Feast*
Thomas Collins: *Ode to Evening*
Elinor Wylie: *Hymn to Earth*
Allen Tate: *Ode to Fear*

The Elegy

An elegy tends to be mournful and often death plays an important role in the subject matter. For example, in Thomas Gray's *Elegy Written in a Country Churchyard* the end of the day, the churchyard yew tree (a symbol of death because of the tree's location, although the origin of the statutory tree was to provide English archers with arrows in times of war) and thoughts of the ultimate destiny of the buried villagers find a place in the subject matter.

Many elegies were written in mourning for a friend who had died:

Percy Bysshe Shelley: *Adonais* (for John Keats)

Alfred Tennyson: *In Memoriam* (for A H Hallam)

Matthew Arnold: *Thyrsis* (for Arthur Hugh Clough)

Gerard Manley Hopkins: *The Wreck of the Deutschland* (for five Fransciscan nuns drowned at sea)

Anthology

Gray, Thomas and Collins, William, *Poetical Works*, ed Roger Lonsdale (1977)

Criticism

Morris, Golden, *Thomas Gray* (1988)

5

NARRATIVE VERSE

As its name suggests, narrative verse tells a story. There is no other criterion. The verse may be of any date and in any form. One of the most popular types of narrative verse is the ballad.

THE BALLAD

Key work: *Lord Randall*

The origin of the ballad is lost in time and various scholars trace different lines of descent. Possibly the form began with a medieval dance or carole, a series of quatrains (four line stanzas) in which the first and third lines represent the narrative sung by the story teller and the remaining two lines are the set refrain, often irrelevant to the story, of the dancers:

> She laid her back against a thorn
> *Fine flowers in the valley,*
> And there she has her sweet babe born
> *And the green leaves they grow rarely.*

When the dance song passed from fashion the refrains were often dropped and the lines filled with an extended narration. Some of the many repetitions found in ballads date from this practice.

Possibly at this stage the ballad was learnt and either sung or recited by a wandering entertainer who, with the process of repetition, sometimes simplified the story. Sir Philip Sidney wrote in the 1580s of a travelling reciter telling the ballad story of *Percy and Douglas*:

> ... it is sung but by some blind crowder with no rougher voice than crude stile; which being so evil apparelled in the dust and cobweb of that uncivil age, what would it work trimmed in the gorgeous eloquence of Pindar?

Pindar was a Greek lyric poet who wrote formal and elevated odes. Sidney's remarks assure us that the ballad was unsophisticated, reflecting in its roughness and violence the times in which it originated.

But what were the ballads about? Some of the ballad stories are part of an international chest of folklore indigenous to Great Britain, Scandinavia and the European continent; other tales are drawn from the Arthurian legend by minstrels during the waning of the middle ages; other minstrels found matter in the sixteenth century in the Robin Hood stories; in the sixteenth and seventeenth centuries local poets composed ballads about the regional history of the Scottish Border country. Numbers of older ballads were tidied and rewritten by Robert Burns and Sir Walter Scott, amongst many others.

Lord Randall, anonymous, serves as an illustration of the ballad tradition.

'O where have you been, Lord Randall, my son?
O where have you been, my handsome young man?'
'I have been to the wild wood; mother, make my
    bed soon,
For I'm weary with hunting, and fain would lie down.'

'Who gave you your dinner, Lord Randall' my son?
Who gave you your dinner, my handsome young man?'
'I dined with my sweetheart; mother, make my bed soon,
For I'm weary with hunting, and fain would lie down.'

'What had you for dinner, Lord Randall, my son?
What had you for dinner, my handsome young man?'
'I had eels boiled in broth; mother, make my bed soon,
For I'm weary with hunting and fain would lie down.'

'And where are your bloodhounds, Lord Randall,
    my son?
And where are your bloodhounds, my handsome
    young man?'

'O they swelled and they died; mother, make my bed soon,
For I'm weary with hunting, and fain would lie down.'

'O I fear you are poisoned, Lord Randall, my son!
O I fear you are poisoned, my handsome young man!'
'O yes! I am poisoned; mother, make my bed soon,
For I'm sick at the heart, and I fain would lie down.'

At this point it would be useful to look at some of the special characteristics of this ballad, compare them with those in other ballads and consider how this relates to the speaking.

The ballad is obviously a conversation between two people, Lord Randall and his mother. It is dramatic in form; no such instructions as 'he said' and 'she said' are needed as this is obvious from the disposition of the lines. Each verse is a repeating pattern; over two lines the mother asks a question and in the two following Randall replies. The dialogue is not in any way naturalistic: a mother does not refer to her son as 'Lord'; she does not speak patterned repeats of phrases; Randall only gives his mother information, his sufferings are not expressed emotionally. Indeed, in this ballad there is neither comment nor moralizing by either person.

In common with other ballads, the story is told by means of the dialogue and a similar content, death by poisoning, is to be found elsewhere. For example, in *Barbara Allen* it is implied that Jemmy Grove has been poisoned.

We get just a hint of the savage world of the ballad in the phrase, 'I have been to the wild wood'; other ballads stress the magical quality of their locations; the first episode of 'True Thomas', for example, takes place under the Eildon Tree, the tree of magic under which a rhymer delivered his prophecies. Magic and mystery is also implied in the groupings of events, people and commodities in either threes (seen as a mystical number because of the Holy Trinity) or sevens (again mystical because seven suggests the manifold: the seven sacraments, the seven deadly sins, and so on). The idea of threeness as expressing imminent disaster is seen in *Sir Patrick Spens*:

> They had not sailed a league, a league,
> A league but barely three,
> When the sky grew dark, the wind blew loud,
> And angry grew the sea.

The rhythm of *Lord Randall* is flexible but throughout each line the four strong beats of the metre can be felt. In this example the lines do not conform to the usual ballad pattern which may be seen in the quoted verse from *Sir Patrick Spens*, four stressed syllables in the first and third lines and three stresses in the alternate lines.

From this information we must extrapolate some pointers towards imaginative speaking. In *Lord Randall* two voices need to be adopted, those of the mother and the poisoned son. This does not necessarily mean that the people will be given characterisations. Instead they may be differentiated by pitch and by the anxiety of the mother and the sickness of Randall. In such a dramatic situation as this one would not cavil if the performer introduced a number of gestures, provided that they were appropriately bold. The direct speech tells the story but not in a naturalistic way: the telling is too spare for that. It proceeds quickly and economically. The pause between each question and its answer is of the shortest. However, each question is different in tone and the intensity of the questioner grows over the first four verses until the mother is able to make her declaration in verse five: 'O I fear you are poisoned...'

When we consider the application of the rhythm of the piece we notice that the questions of the mother easily carry the four stresses to the line; their propellation helps to convey the urgency of the questions. In each stanza the first line of Randall poses rhythmic problems. In the third line of the first verse if the strong beat were entirely regular, it could be maintained that the stresses fall thus:

> i have BEEN to the WILD wood; mother, MAKE
> my bed SOON

However the importance of some words compete with this metrical pattern. In the description of the location (an important point because it is one of the few indications of the dangerous, medieval kind of landscape found in ballads) 'wild wood', is the adjective 'wild' really more important than the noun 'wood'? Move the stress from 'wild' to 'WOOD' and you get an interesting kind of cross rhythm. I have not mentioned unstressed syllables because the number of these is often variable in ballads, a hint of the flexibility of memorised spoken epics.

The third line of the third stanza is obviously regular:

i had EELS boiled in BROTH

and the corresponding line of the fourth verse is a baleful reflection of the former verse:

o they SWELLED and they DIED...

The last stanza contains the acknowledgement:

O YES! i am POIsoned

and I'm suggesting that the first foot is in the nature of a spondee in order to emphasise this realization. 'O' is a word not used in speaking today and some candidates fail to give the vowel its full poetic value: use it and, without being indulgent, exploit it.

The phrase 'mother, make my bed soon' is repeated in each stanza and the reason for the phrase differs several times: Randall speaks this on one occasion because he is weary, then because he is feeling ill, and the nature of the request changes when he admits to his realisation that he has been poisoned. This, therefore is more than just a chorus; its changing subtext needs to be stated in the speaking but nevertheless you must work within the confines of the rhythmic pattern. The problem is to decide how much stress to give to the metrical beat and whether the text implies that an inverted foot has been introduced.

Do you stand or sit to speak a ballad? Various candidates would differ in their approach. One will see the dramatic potential of the poem and feel that a number of stances and the occasional gesture suits his interpretation whilst another will wish to give a less flamboyant presentation, sitting and making this in essence a story. The narrator is distancing himself from the action in this case. Whatever is decided on, a rough, homespun quality must be brought to the fore and the economy of words and pace of the narrative (already mentioned) must be respected.

A selection of ballads

Barbara Allen

Edward, Edward

Sir Patrick Spens

The Wife of Usher's Well

W H Auden: *Victor. A Ballad*

Samuel Taylor Coleridge: *The Rime of the Ancient Mariner*

William Cowper: *The Diverting History of John Gilpin*

W S Gilbert: *The Yarn of the Nancy Bell*

A E Houseman: *The True Lover*

J M Synge: *Danny*

Vernon Watkins: *The Ballad of Culver's Hole*

Oscar Wilde: *The Ballad of Reading Gaol*

Anthologies containing selections of ballads

Herbert, David, ed, *Penguin Book of Narrative Verse* (1960)

Untermeyer, Louis, ed, *Collins' Albatross Book of Verse* (1933)

Books on the ballad

Bold, Alan, *The Ballad* (1971)

Harris, Joseph, *The Ballad and Oral Literature* (1991)

OTHER NARRATIVE VERSE

Key work: *Badger* by John Clare

The term 'narrative verse' covers a range of work; many tales are told, the narrative style differs and the form of the various poems is shaped to assist in the telling.

I want to use an example of narrative verse and extrapolate from that a number of general points. In contrast with the anonymous ballad, here is an excerpt from *Badger*, by John Clare, the Northamptonshire country poet, who gazed with great pleasure on the natural world surrounding him.

> When midnight comes a host of dogs and men
> Go out and track the badger to his den,
> And put a sack within the hole, and lie
> Till the old grunting badger passes by.
> He comes and hears – they let the strongest loose.
> The old fox hears the noise and drops the goose.
> The poacher shoots and hurries from the cry,
> And the old hare half wounded buzzes by.
> They get a forked stick to bear him down
> And clap the dogs and take him to the town,
> And bait him all the day with many dogs,
> And laugh and shout and fright the scampering hogs.
> He runs along and bites at all he meets:
> They shout and hollo down the noisy streets.
>
> He turns about to face the loud uproar
> And drives the rebels to their very door.
> The frequent stone is hurled where'er they go;
> When badgers fight, then every one's a foe.
> The dogs are clapped and urged to join the fray;
> The badger turns and drives them all away
> Though scarcely half as big, demure and small,
> He fights with dogs for hours and beats them all.
> The heavy mastiff, savage in the fray,
> Lies down and licks his feet and turns away.
> The bulldog knows his match and waxes cold,

The badger grins and never leaves his hold.
He drives the crowd and follows at their heels
And bites them through – the drunkard swears and reels.

The frighted women take the boys away,
The blackguard laughs and hurries on the fray.
He tries to reach the woods, an awkward race,
But sticks and cudgels quickly stop the chace.
He turns again and drives the noisy crowd
And beats the many dogs in noises loud.
He drives away and beats them every one,
And then they loose them all and set them on.
He falls as dead and kicked by boys and men,
Then starts and grins and drives the crowd agen;
Till kicked and torn and beated out he lies
And leaves his hold and cackles, groans, and dies.

John Clare's patient observation is ploughed back into the telling of this story. He delights in small details and as you read the piece you probably realised that much of the visuals in the poem are from the badger's viewpoint rather than at a human eye-level. Nevertheless, Clare is not making a protest in this poem, nor is he overtly sad at the harrying and death of the badger; in fact he refers to him as 'the blackguard' and draws attention to the danger that all of life could be in:

When badgers fight, then every one's a foe.

For your part, it would not be suitable to introduce anger or compassion and certainly not sentiment for it is your purpose to convey what the poet has to say, not your own opinions. That is one clue to the tone of the speaking.

Another is the choice of language the poet uses in his story telling. This is very simple, direct stuff, in fact it is surprising how many words of only one syllable are used, as in the line:

And bait him all the day with many dogs...

The diction of the poem is always an accurate pointer to the way in which we should speak. This must be forthright, unglossed by too much use of inflection and without any conscious colouring of words. There is a pleasure and satisfaction in the hurly-burly of country life for Clare which the speaker, hopefully, conveys.

In a narrative it is wise to decide at which point in the story occurs the climax or highlight of the piece. Each stanza seems to have an important moment. In the first it is the noise of dogs, hogs and people; stanza two works towards the havoc the badger causes as he chases the crowd; the success of the dogs in killing the badger seems a natural climax of the third stanza. For me the principal hot spot would be the unleashing of all the dogs halfway through the last verse. By that time the death of the badger is an inevitability. The poem needs to gain in impetus as one nears each of these climaxes, with the greatest gain in the last. Such a mounting of pace helps to give the listener the feeling that the narrative is getting somewhere, that the speaker knows where he is taking his audience. However, do make sure that any changes in pace are controlled. A sudden acceleration can be a distraction. When I'm preparing a piece for performance I usually look at the way in which I am going to rise to the climaxes and then, through de-acceleration, decide on the overall pace of the poem.

Guides to the pace here are the metrical pattern and the rhyming scheme. Each line has five main stresses running through it:

and PUT a SACK withIN the HOLE, and LIE

telling us that each line is composed of five imabic feet. Occasionally Clare makes a telling alteration to the pattern. The reversal and consequent change of rhythm in the line:

TILL the old GRUNTing badger passes by

well expresses the lumbering gait of the creature. Look out for other examples of rhythmic change and try to understand why Clare introduces these.

The rhyme scheme is simplicity itself, with the poem consisting of couplets. In speaking, be careful not to land heavily on the rhyming words. These rhyming couplets help to imprint the pattern of the verse on the mind of the listener and so it is not necessary to draw attention to unstopped line endings with suspensory pauses. The strength of rhythm and the simplicity of rhyme will ensure that a clear picture of the pattern is conveyed. The first four lines could well be spoken on a single breath as only the merest hints of pauses are needed at the commas. However, after the fourth line a pause of expectation is needed. The dash after 'He comes and hears' signifies another pause but then one needs to catch up on the rhythm in the remainder of the line. Although two stanza pauses are necessary, don't make them too long. The movement of the verse needs to be pushed forward. Certainly no rallentando is required at the end of stanzas 1 and 2. The separation of the last words of the poem, 'and cackles, groans, and dies' creates a slowing down which is needed to give the required emphasis on the final word.

I've already mentioned that Clare does not seem to take sides in this fight to the death, although the focus of the poem is on the badger. So during the affrays between the various dogs in the second stanza no kind of colouring is necessary: you are giving a commentary and the listener sorts out his own responses to this. There is a harshness in the poem, especially as Clare uses the world as seen by the badger, a place of sticks (twice mentioned) and kicks and hurled stones; this harshness sets the tone for the speaker. There are two passing vignettes of dogs, the mastiff and the bulldog, and you can well be appreciative about the qualities of these but again without sentimentality. Clare's view of the natural world is very different from our own and to try to introduce modern susceptibilities into this would work against the given text.

Anthologies of John Clare's poetry

Clare, John, *Selected Poems*, ed Geoffrey Grigson (1950)

Clare, John, *Selected Poems*, ed James Reeves (1954)

Books on John Clare

Storey, Mark, *The Poetry of John Clare, a Critical Introduction* (1974)
Tibble, J W and A, *John Clare: his Life and Poetry* (1956)

Collection

The Peterborough Museum and Art Gallery houses the John Clare Collection; a descriptive catalogue is available.

A selection of narrative poems

Some of the following are too long for examination purposes but there is no reason why you should not fillet out a suitable excerpt.

Robert Browning: *The Pied Piper of Hamelin*
G K Chesterton: *Lepanto*
George Crabbe: *Peter Grimes*
John Gay: *The Rat-Catcher and the Cats*
Robert Greene: *Mars and Venus*
James Kirkup: *A Correct Compassion*
Edward Lear: *The Jumblies*
Alun Lewis: *All Day it has Rained*
Christopher Logue: *The Song of the Dead Soldier*
Walter de la Mare: *Goliath*
John Masefield: *Reynard the Fox*
Alfred Noyes: *The Highwayman*
Wilfred Owen: *The Sentry*

A few volumes of narrative verse

Chaucer, Geoffrey, *The Canterbury Tales*, ed A C Cawley (1958)
Herbert, David, *The Penguin Book of Narrative Verse* (1960)
Opie, Iona, ed, *The Oxford Book of Narrative Verse* (1989)
Tolkien, J R R, *The Lays of Beleriand* (1985)

Article

Melville, Sonia, *Tell Me A Story* in *Speech and Drama* volume 45, number 1 (1996)

RECAPITULATION: PREPARING AND SPEAKING A POEM

In this and the three previous chapters you have been studying the process involved in preparing and speaking a poem. It seems advisable to make a summary of the stages which have been recommended.

These first points relate to the preparation of the poem:

- read through the poem several times and jot down your immediate personal responses; when familiarity has staled the poem, your notes are a useful reminder of some responses which must be conveyed in the speaking

- consider carefully why the poem has been given the title it bears. Sometimes this is solely factual and may be taken at its face value as in *The Priory of St Saviour, Glendalough.* At other times the title is a pun which either seriously or humourously introduces the reader to new aspects of a subject. This is made evident in *Road Signs: Diversion Ahead.* The poet, P M Nixon, equates 'diversion' with 'an amusement':

  Will it be clowns, I wonder,
  Staggering around the hard shoulder
  On stilts?

- consider the content. Names new to you, whether of people or places, will have to be researched. Many candidates speak the following lines in Seamus Heaney's poem *Blackberry-Picking*:

  Our hands were peppered
  With thorn pricks, our palms sticky as
  Bluebeard's.

  Strangely, they do not realise that Bluebeard murdered his wives and his hands are sticky with their blood. One can tell by the lyrical way in which his name is spoken that the background research has not been done. You may also come across new ideas and here again you have to grapple. Helen Spalding has written a poem *Let us Now Praise Prime Numbers* in which she presents not only mathematical terms but also the concepts behind them. It would be difficult to speak this poem with conviction if you had not mastered these. One gradually comes to terms with the meaning of a poem; take your time and allow the intricacies gradually to sink into your consciousness

- undertake some research on the poet and the physical conditions in which he lived and worked. Living poets need to be researched too. Discover the circumstances in which the poem you are studying came to be written: Gerard Manley Hopkins, for example, wrote *The Wreck of the Deutschland* when he heard in 1875 that the ship the *Deutschland* had sunk in the mouth of the Thames and that five Franciscan nuns, exiled by the Falck Laws, had been drowned. This news affected him so deeply he channelled his feelings into a long, elaborate elegy;

- discover the intention of the poet in writing his poem. Candidates do not always realise that a piece is not to be taken at its face value: it may be an ironical statement. *The Lesson* by Roger McGough is often spoken as if it were a disaster poem; I think it is more than this as it questions many values. Once you feel that you have fully understood the intention behind the writing look at the tone of the poem. This is going to affect the tone of your speaking. Listen to the voice of the poet and make sure that when you are speaking a poem his voice may be heard. I don't mean listen to a recording and try to reproduce the voice of, say, John Betjeman. The challenge is sharper than this. In the quiet and prosaic writing of Philip Larkin is a world of muted happiness, pain, and the implied question, 'What's the worth of this

kind of life?' I'm sure if you look at Larkin's poem
Days you can hear the voice behind the words:

> What are days for?
> Days are where we live.
> They come, they wake us
> Time and time over.
> They are to be happy in:
> Where can we live but days?
>
> Ah, solving that question
> Brings the priest and the doctor
> In their long coats
> Running over the fields.

- work on the technical aspects of the poem:

  * look carefully at the structure of your poem
    and see how the poet uses this to get his material
    across to the reader or listener

  * think about the principal climax and the sub-
    climaxes and the way in which you are going
    to bring these to the fore without force or fuss

  * look at the rhyming scheme; this too is often
    a means of sectionalising a poem

  * think about the various sections and divisions;
    consider to what extent you must bring these
    to the attention of your audience

  * think of the rhythm and how this is going to
    determine the pace of your speaking (content,
    intensity, elaboration, complications in the
    writing are also determinants of the pace)

  * word quality must be studied, but the old rule
    for church flower arrangers holds here, 'Don't
    decorate the decorated!'

  * consider the dynamics you are to use and the
    ways of moving across the dynamic range

- be aware of the technical demands the poem makes on you. We have already seen that in order to speak authoritatively Gerald Manley Hopkins' poems we need to have an insight into his understanding of sprung rhythm; that is only one technical demand. Some poems make great demands on our breathing, others on our range of speaking

- think of the way in which you can use your visual appearance in the presentation of the poem: will you stand, sit, lie on the floor? How will your clothes affect the presentation of the piece?

When you perform the poem the following may be considered:

- announce the title; vocal tone must suggest something of the spirit of the ensuing work; judge the length of your pause before starting the verse, for the audience needs to be able to make an appraisal of their expectations;

- when you are performing don't dwell on technical matters. All of your attention must be on transmitting the poem, its content, its tone, the voice of the poet

- be careful not to outstare the examiner and don't glaze over. Choose a point in front of you to look at; changes of eye focus are necessary and can help one to grasp the content; occasionally look directly at the examiner

- when you have finished the poem, don't be too eager to leave it; quietly savour the effect of the poem for a moment and allow the examiner to do the same.

This is a formidable list. Don't be over-awed by it. The aim is merely to help you to speak a poem and to enjoy both the speaking and the preparation which preceded it.

6

SPEAKING PROSE

In this chapter I will give a set of guidelines on speaking prose and then consider two examples in the light of these. A prose selection may, of course, be either an excerpt from a novel or an example of non-fiction writing, and obviously a wide range of material is available in the latter set. For example, many journals, diaries or letters, a personal non-fiction genre, provide an illuminating insight into the life and thought of a writer.

PREPARATORY READING

Read the complete work from which you are going to select a suitable piece. As you read, note any sections of the book which may be appropriate for performance. In choosing a piece your aim will be to give an adequate idea of the book and also to reveal your own ability to handle prose as well as verse. A point to consider in your selection is whether the piece is obviously written to be spoken by a man or a woman. This depends on how personal the writing is. For example, some parts of the published letters of Virginia Woolf would be only suitable for a woman speaker. On the other hand, sometimes a person is such an established character in the collective mind of a nation – Dr Samuel Johnson or Queen Victoria – that his or her writing would sit uneasily on the lips of a member of the opposite sex.

TONE

You need to assess the tone of the complete book and, looking at your chosen excerpt, decide to what extent this reflects it. Sometimes differences in tone are obvious: P G Wodehouse writes his novels with a jocularity which prompts one to laugh aloud but in contrast Jane Austen, although the novels are witty and on occasion strongly humorous, brings a warmth to the heart rather than a guffaw from the belly. Sometimes the tone of an excerpt depends on the period in which it was written: the letters of Horace Walpole in their eighteenth-century urbanity are very precise and technical expertise is needed in the speaking. This is evident in the short jabs of prose in which Walpole describes the London earthquake of 1750:

> I got up and found people running into the streets, but saw no mischief done: there has been some; two old houses flung down, several chimneys and much chinaware. The bells rung in several houses.

In addition to the precision, there is also humour in the face of danger in his afterthought about the china and the servants' bells ringing themselves. This excerpt illustrates the importance of discovering information about the writer of the selected work as well as about his times and literary background. One also has to ask: 'Why has the author written this work?'. A book may be appreciated on several different levels and through his skill the speaker may be able to take his audience to the deepest of these. *Gulliver's Travels* is often enjoyed by younger readers as an adventure story; Jonathan Swift wrote the book for an adult readership able to discern the satire in his work.

When considering the tone of excerpts from the Bible, be aware that the translation may make a difference. Sometimes I get students to look at St Mark's Gospel, chapter 16, verse 6. The context is that three woman have arrived at the sepulchre in which the body of Jesus has been buried to anoint him with oil and herbs. They find the door of the tomb rolled back and a white-robed young man sitting inside. He speaks to them and in the *Authorized Version* (published during the reign of James I) his words are given:

> Be not amazed: ye seek Jesus the Nazarene, which hath been crucified: he is risen; he is not here: behold, the place where they laid him!

This is obviously a joyful proclamation, but it is also dignified and reserved. Let us look at just the opening three words of this in some other translations. The *Jerusalem Bible* makes the text more immediate but some of the mystery is lost in its 'There is no need for alarm'; the *New English Bible*, tending to be more formal than the *Jerusalem Bible*, gives the man's command as 'Fear nothing'; the *Good News Bible* has 'Don't be alarmed', very informal but hardly appropriate for a mysterious event of great importance. In the *Jerusalem Bible* and the *Good News Bible* there is a decided change of tone from the wording in the *Authorized Version* and the *New English Bible*. The three more recent translations have been made within the past fifty years.

SHAPING

Once you have decided on your excerpt, study this in order to discover where the highlight, or climax, of the piece occurs. In a description of a car chase, for example, this may be the point at which one of the cars falls over the edge of the motorway. Have another look, and decide whether there are any sub-climactic moments. Once these have been identified you have then to consider how you are going to lead the listener to the climax. An increase of pace and dynamics may help. Where suspense occurs a diminution of the dymanic range can help the listener to appreciate the threatening terror in the situation. Possibly at the end of your piece you will need some kind of de-crescendo as you take the audience down onto firm ground.

EDITING

Occasionally a piece requires editing if it is to be spoken to the greatest effect. The writer may make a back-reference which is not needed in the selection or other kinds of unwanted interjection may occur. A listener is not a reader, he cannot refer to the text to clarify a point. The clarifying is done through the editing and the speaking.

Parts of the text may be superfluous for a speaker. In a novel, for example, such directional words as 'John said' may be dispensed with, especially when the speaker is able clearly to differentiate between several speakers. Advice on this is given under 'Dialogue'.

RHYTHM

Having studied the excerpt carefully, by this time you will no doubt be aware that prose can be rhythmical, as is verse. The rhythm may be used by the speaker to help in the presentation: fluency and pace are often dependent on it. The following is a description taken from *Tess of the d'Urbervilles* by Thomas Hardy of a prospect of Wintoncester (in reality Winchester) seen from the top of the West Hill. In this long, rambling sentence listen for the inherent rhythm which both moves and clarifies the text:

> In the valley beneath lay the city they had just left, its more prominent buildings showing as in an isometric drawing – among them the broad cathedral tower, with its Norman windows and immense length of aisle and nave, the spires of St Thomas's, the pinnacled tower of the College, and, more to the right, the tower and gables of the ancient hospice, where to this day the pilgrim may receive his dole of bread and ale.

Rhythm can reverberate through an oratorical work. The repetitions and the pattern of the two questions followed by their measured answers is an indication of the power of Winston Churchill's speeches in the early days of the Second World War:

> You ask, What is our policy? I will say: it is to wage war, by sea, land, and air, with all our might and with all the strength that God can give us: to wage war against a monstrous tyranny, never surpassed in the dark, lamentable catalogue of human crime. That is our policy. You ask, What is our aim? I can answer in one word: Victory – victory at all costs, victory in spite of all terror; victory, however long and hard the road may be; for without victory there is no survival.

PACE

When I was a child the advice given for presenting a prose excerpt was: 'You must speak this slowly enough to manage the text and fast enough to maintain the interest of the audience'. That is basic good advice. However, there is more to a consideration of pace than this. The subject matter in part determines the pace of an excerpt: the difference in pace between a description of the funeral of Mary Tudor and the commentary on the finish of a horse race is obvious. The period in which the novel is set also influences the pace. An excerpt from *A Clockwork Orange* (post 1962) by Anthony Burgess with its fictional language and degrading violence will be taken at a very different pace than paragraphs from Ivy Compton-Burnett's *A Family and a Fortune* (high Victorian setting) with its decorous manners and the writer's love of meal-time conversations.

Often pace suffers from a speaker's misplaced desire to over-colour the text. Towards the end of his life Emlyn Williams' readings from the novels of Charles Dickens were tediously slow. Most adjectives and adverbs will look after themselves and there is no need to draw attention to them. Pace sometimes seems pedestrian because the speaker has not learnt the art of 'throwing away' relatively unimportant word clusters in the text:

John Martin, I have to say, was useless at cabinet making.

'I have to say' contains next to no information and this phrase may be spoken more rapidly than the rest of the sentence. Sometimes words appear in parenthesis in a sentence but they are obviously important:

Then we saw the man – crazed with evil and a desire
for revenge, he had procured a knife – and we knew
at once that the Police must be warned.

The technique of dealing with such an interjection is to pause momentarily at the start, lower the pitch slightly and speak the interrupting words a little faster but giving full weight to the key words. These slight variations in pace will lighten the speaking and maintain interest in the narration.

DIALOGUE

These are a few lines from a short story by Oscar Wilde entitled *The Birthday of the Infanta*:

> ...the little dwarf never looked up, and his sobs grew fainter and fainter, and suddenly he gave a curious gasp, and clutched his side. And then he fell back again, and lay quite still.

> 'That is capital,' said the Infanta, after a pause; 'but now you must dance for me.'

> 'Yes,' cried all the children, 'you must get up and dance, for you are as clever as the Barbary apes, and much more ridiculous.'

> But the little dwarf made no answer.

> And the Infanta stamped her foot, and called out to her uncle, who was walking on the terrace with the Chamberlain, reading some dispatches that had just arrived from Mexico, where the Holy Office had recently been established. 'My funny little dwarf is sulking,' she cried, 'you must wake him up and tell him to dance for me.'

In this passage the direct speech of a number of people is recorded and this poses challenges for the speaker. First amongst these is the speaking of the Infanta, a twelve year old princess, spoilt and heartless. Contrasted with hers are the voices of the common children with whom the princess was allowed to play for one day each year. There is, of course, another voice, that of the narrator.

The speaker must make a decision. Are the voices, with the exception of the narrator's, to be given so distinct a personality that they are characterised and the story has the quality of a radio play with some intermittent comment from the narrator or are they merely to be differentiated by some technical means, such as a slight raising of the pitch for the Infanta's speaking? Either method is acceptable and the content of the material, as so often, must suggest to the speaker the suitability of his approach. Assuming the first method is used, the speaker must be very careful that the acquisition of voices does not hold up the pace. The audience is anxious to know how the plot is progressing as much as to be entertained by a gallery of characters. The speaker must switch with rapidity from the narration to the demanding, higher pitched voice of the child and then with equal ease return to the narration. He must, too, cut into the dialogue very rapidly with the stage directions, if used, at such points as 'cried all the children'. There must be a balance of tone and dynamics amongst the various character voices and that of the narrator. A balance too must be maintained within the story as a whole: one of the characters at a moment of agitation must not break the vocal tenor which has been set. There is the additional responsibility to ensure that the narrator's voice is truly the natural voice of the speaker but which remains uninvolved in the action, offering comment and guidance to the listener from an objective distance. The second of the two approaches mentioned above is the more bland, nevertheless, in a realistic story with few voices entering into the narrative, it can work very well indeed and increase the cohesion of the writing.

Whichever method is used, pauses are an important part of telling the story. A dramatic pause is needed, for example, at the end of the bitterly sad sentence, 'But the little dwarf made no answer'.

Telling a story is an exercise in the 'Technique of the Three Ps': Pace, Pitch and Pause.

Your story-telling may be smoother if some judicious cutting is made to the text. For examination purposes this will usually be minimal. In the Wilde selection, for example, after the Princess has said 'That is capital' is the note 'after a pause' necessary? You as the speaker are able to demonstrate this. In the last sentence 'she cried' is superfluous if you can create the speech of the Infanta.

PERSONAL PROSE

By 'personal prose' I mean such writing as diaries, letters and journals. These convey much of the personality of the writer and they are usually free of dialogue in the conventional sense, although some would claim that a diary is an extended monologue. This poses the problem, 'To what extent do I characterize the speaking?' It is impossible to give a general answer: each occasion depends on appropriateness. For example, if the diary were that of an isolated country woman living on a small-holding in the west of Ireland, then obviously dialect would be needed. The performer primarily has to give the listener the feeling that Parson Woodforde, John Evelyn, Evelyn Waugh, Samuel Pepys, or whoever the diarist is, is speaking.

THE SPEAKER IN PERFORMANCE

In a previous section the speaker was confronted with decisions to be made about the extent of his vocal involvement in the passage; here he must come to terms with his physical involvement in the story. I often recommend my own students to stay sitting for the story, as the narrator has to be as relaxed as possible. Some gesture, provided it arises naturally, may be made at moments of excitement but most of the time the speaker is reasonably still. Occasionally, if the story is highly active, it is appropriate to stand and then some minor movement – but keep this within a compact area – may be made as well as gestures. However, the performance must hang together; the audience is not to be left with the impression that at one moment it is watching a highly dramatic play and at another listening to a narration. It is for this reason that I feel it is unwise to change from a sitting position to a standing in the process of telling a story because the audience needs to make too many adjustments.

Sometimes I'm asked, 'Who do I tell the story to?' – a question which really means 'What is the direction of my speaking?' Don't transfix the examiner with a glazed stare: this will discomfort him and make you appear stilted. Imagine that the examiner is just one person in an audience which ranges to the sides of him and behind him. Then you can tell your story to various members of this imaginary audience, directing different parts to different people.

Key text: *Dracula* by Bram Stoker

The first of the two key texts which I will examine is from Bram Stoker's horror novel *Dracula* and I envisage this as a suitable piece for a Bronze Medal candidate. I have edited slightly the following text in preparation for speaking:

> I heard a heavy step approaching behind the great door, and saw through the chinks the gleam of a coming light. Then there was the sound of rattling chains and the clanking of massive bolts drawn back. A key was turned with the loud grating noise of long disuse, and the great door swung back.

> Within, stood a tall old man, clean-shaven save for a long white moustache, and clad in black from head to foot, without a single speck of colour about him anywhere. He held in his hand an antique silver lamp, in which the flame burned without chimney or globe of any kind, throwing long, quivering shadows as it flickered in the draught of the open door. The old man motioned me in with his right hand with a courtly gesture, saying in excellent English, but with a strange intonation:

> 'Welcome to my house! Enter freely and of your own will!' He made no motion of stepping to meet me, but stood like a statue, as though his gesture of welcome had fixed him into stone. The instant, however, that I stepped over the threshold, he moved impulsively forward, and holding out his hand grasped mine with

a strength which made me wince, an effect which was not lessened by the fact that it seemed as cold as ice – more like the hand of a dead than a living man. Again he said:-

'Welcome to my house. Come freely. Go safely. And leave something of the happiness you bring!' The strength of the handshake was so much akin to that which I had noticed in the driver that for a moment I doubted if it were not the same person to whom I was speaking; so, to make sure, I said interrogatively:-

'Count Dracula?' He bowed in a courtly way as he replied:

'I am Dracula.'

Bram Stoker wrote *Dracula* in 1897 and the setting is contemporary with the writing. The somewhat formal style is explained by the fact that this excerpt is taken from Jonathan Harker's journal; the whole novel is in the form of diaries and letters. The writing is also dramatic. Not for nothing was Stoker a theatre critic and tour manager to Sir Henry Irving, the great Victorian actor. The plot tells of the blood-drinking vampire Dracula, almost five hundred years old, one of the 'undead' of German folklore and this gives the book a dark and horrific tone. Harker has undertaken a long and perilous journey to Transylvania to meet Dracula at his mountain retreat surrounded by baying wolves and this is his first face-to-face confrontation with the count. Subsequent dramatisations of *Dracula* have sometimes introduced a vein of self-mockery into the presentation but this would be totally inappropriate in a performance based directly on Stoker's text.

The excerpt seems to me to be divided into two sections. The first part is the shorter of the two and consists of Jonathan Harker (and also the listener) waiting for a figure to open the door to the castle. The second part consists of one's first impressions of the strange person who eventually appears and the gradual realisation that this is Count Dracula himself. There are therefore two points to which the speaker should drive the narration: firstly to the words 'the great door swung back' at the end of the first paragraph and secondly to the count's dramatic but simple revelation at the end of the excerpt, 'I am Dracula'. In order to build up the suspense the speaker may slightly stretch the last sentence of the first paragraph, following this by a decided pause before going on to describe the figure in the aperture. Dracula's final remark requires deliberate speaking as he lays curiosity to rest.

In reading the excerpt you have probably realised that the dialogue has its own rhythm. Harker says remarkably little and his sole question is tersely put. Dracula is more forthcoming but his sentences are short and simple. These snippets of direct speech contrast with the longer sentences of the narrative, a point to note in speaking. Indeed, some of the sentences are extended and urgent and the speaker must use his supply of breath wisely in order to maintain projection to the full stop.

The listener wants to learn much about Harker through his narrative and so a youthful, heroic presence must come to the fore, depending on variety and directness of speaking but devoid of vocal tricks. Count Dracula is very different. Here he is on home ground and seemingly welcoming to Harker although soon he will hold him a prisoner in his castle. The voice of Dracula suggests firstly his extreme age and his veneer of courtesy but at the same time the performer must leave the listener feeling uneasy, for Dracula lacks integrity.

Earlier I explained that I had lightly edited the text in order to make it cohesive. There are still several phrases, however, notably those which precede sections of dialogue ('Again he said' and 'I said interrogatively') which you may consider cutting.

You have yet to think about your use of the performance space and your position when speaking the excerpt. These are matters of right judgement – no mechanical rules can be applied – and I have to leave you to make your own decisions on these matters.

Key text: *The Bell* by Iris Murdoch

The second of the chosen key texts is selected from *The Bell*, by Iris Murdoch. This is a novel of some complexity offering a suitable challenge for a Gold Medal or Diploma candidate.

> The station was just outside the village on the Imber side. A lane with high overgrown hedges wound across the fields, and the footpath to Imber left it a quarter of a mile further on. Dora wondered whether to cross the line and go into the village. But there was no point in it, since the pubs would not be open yet. She turned into the dark tunnel of the lane. The sound of the train and the car had died away. A murmur accompanied her steps, which must come from a tiny stream invisible in the ditch. She walked on, her hands in her pockets.
>
> Her hand encountered the envelope which Paul had given her. She drew it out fearfully. It would have to be something unpleasant. She opened it.
>
> It contained two brief letters, both written by herself. The first one, which she saw dated from the early days of their engagement, read as follows:
>
>> Dear *dear* Paul, it was so wonderful last night and such absolute pain to leave you. I lay awake fretting for you. I can't wait for tonight, so am dropping this in at the library. It's agony to go away from you, and so wonderful to think that soon we shall be much more together. Wanting to be with you always, dearest Paul, ever ever ever your loving Dora.
>
> Dora perused this missive, and then looked at the other one, which read as follows:

Paul, I can't go on. It's been so awful lately, and awful for you too, I know. So I'm leaving – leaving you. I can't stay and you know all the reasons why. I know I'm a wretch and it's all my fault, but I can't stand it and I can't stay. Forgive this scrappy note. When you get it I'll be finally gone. Don't try to get me back and don't bother about the things I've left. I've taken what I need. Dora.

P.S. I'll write again later, but I won't have anything else to say than this.

This was the note Dora had left at Knightsbridge on the day she departed. Shaken, she re-read both letters. She folded them up and walked on. So Paul carried them always in his wallet and wanted to have them back to go on carrying them. So much the worse for Paul. Dora tore the letters into small fragments and strewed them along the hedge.

Iris Murdoch's novel reveals to the reader a tangled web of relationships. Two of the main characters are Paul and Dora Greenfield. Once Dora had left her husband Paul because she was afraid of him and then, afraid of him still, she decided to return. Much of the action takes place in the village of Imber. One of its institutions is a convent where an austere order of nuns live; in the shadow of this is a rambling house in which a group of lay people for their part experiment in community living. Paul and Dora have attempted to throw in their lot here.

A cursory reading would convey the tone. In colour terms it is grey; there is the bleak wildness of the countryside, the closed pubs, the isolation of Dora and the certainty that the relationship has ended. Expressed in the plain bleak sentence, 'So much the worse for Paul,' this is the climax of the excerpt it seems to me.

The remainder consists of two excursions into the past through the medium of letters. The first letter is one of hope and passion written near to the start of the relationship, preserved by Paul over many years. The second letter heralds the break.

How do these points relate to speaking? Although the narrator is a person outside the emotional field, here he must still convey the greyness of tone through a vocal sadness. Obviously this cannot be unalleviated throughout and the two letters help to give vocal variety. Murdoch gives Dora a literary style of her own: she tends to emphasize through pairs rather than single statements, for example, 'it was so wonderful last night and such absolute pain to leave you'. This idiosyncrasy needs to be brought out lightly in the speaking but to take this as far as a characterization of Dora would here be an intrusion into the narration. The first letter, of course, is redolent with passion and joy and this can be used. The second is determined – and this again offers a note of contrast – as Dora decides to make the break with Paul.

In the final paragraph comes the fateful sentence, 'So much the worse for Paul'. The preceding three sentences prepare for this one. When it comes, what then? Murdoch has been helpful. Each word consists of a single syllable with the quality of the knell of a funeral bell (the title and subject of the book); the sentence, too, may be broken down into three iambic feet: it is highly rhythmic, weighted, ready for the speaker to stress.

The pace throughout is changing. The quoted letters each have a pace of their own, consonant with the overall rate at which the excerpt is spoken. What are the characteristics of the prose which help you to determine the pace in the sections portioned to the narrator? The first paragraph is written in short, very simple sentences consisting either of a new scrap of information or a succession of actions. This suggests that the speaking could be reasonably rapid with a sparseness of colouring. Each sentence needs to stand complete so that punctuation pauses are clean cut and brief.

When considering the physical presentation one has to query whether sitting will be more helpful than standing. The note of quietness in Iris Murdoch's writing would certainly be underlined if the speaker sat to perform this excerpt. The presentation should be informal and one needs to feel the intimacy of the audience so that the narrator may become a sympathetic guide to this stage of the story of a relationship.

Resources

In my own recitals I've used excerpts from the novels and short stories of the authors listed below. They all have the ability to write prose which bears speaking aloud:

Jane Austen, William Burgess, Ivy Compton-Burnett, G K Chesterton, Charles Dickens, Graham Greene, Thomas Hardy, P D James, Iris Murdoch, Barbara Pym, William Trevor, Oscar Wilde.

Many letters conveying their writers' personalities may also be spoken effectively. The following provide useful material:

Aitken, James, ed, *English Letters of the Eighteenth Century* (1946)
Bennett, Arnold, *Letters of Arnold Bennett*, ed James Hepburn (1986)
Kenyon, Olga, ed, *Eight Hundred Years of Women's Letters* (1992)
Wedgwood, Josiah, *The Selected Letters of Josiah Wedgwood*, ed Ann Finer and George Savage (1965)

Journals and diaries are more personal than letters unless they are written with the intention of an eventual publication. Here are a few suggestions:

Asquith, Cynthia, *Diaries 1915 – 1918* (1968)
Jarman, Derek, *Modern Nature. The Journals of Derek Jarman* (1991)
Kilvert, Francis, *Kilvert's Diary*, ed William Plommer (1977)
Pepys, Samuel, *The Shorter Pepys*, ed Robert Latham (1986)
Woodforde, James, *A Country Parson. James Woodforde's Diary. 1759 – 1802*, ed James Michie (1985)

Excerpts from essays, chosen with discrimination, also make for interesting speaking:

Addison, Joseph and Steele, Richard, *The Spectator*, ed Donald F Bond (1965)
Williams, W E, ed, *A Book of English Essays* (1942)
Woolf, Virginia, *Collected Essays* (1967)

As a source for examples of high oratory I'd mention:

Churchill, Winston, *Into Battle*, ed Randolph S Churchill
   (1941)
Churchill, Winston, *Onwards to Victory*, ed Charles Eade
   (1944)

The above list consists of a few suggestions and indications. Your own reading interests will lead you to many other possibilities.

7

PREPARED READING, VERSE AND PROSE

Many of the points made in dealing with the performance of pre-learnt verse and prose apply here so it would be a good idea to look through these relevant earlier sections in this book. The main differences are that one has not totally learnt the work, although in the preparation much will be retained in mind, and that therefore a script is needed. My concern in this brief chapter is how to deal with the script.

Always provide a stiff cover in which to place your script. Any slight nervousness makes our hands shake and this then causes the pieces of paper to flutter and rustle. A stiffened folder will prevent the apparency of any tremblings. A ring binder is useful to ensure that the pages are held securely within the folder.

Most candidates whom I meet stand and hold the script to give a reading and this can be the least helpful position to the speaker. A lectern is the ideal and a simple wooden travelling one can be made to use in the examination. A music stand, provided it is stable enough and tall enough, makes a good substitute. Try not to hide behind the lectern but rather stand to one side of it, so that the whole body can be seen. If you have to use a table lectern, move it to the corner of the table nearest to you but remember that these are awkward and the height can rarely be adjusted. Failing the provision of a lectern I would recommend that you sit to give the reading. Let the text guide you.

Your aim in reading is to bring the writer to the listener and it is necessary to make easy contact with the latter. This means that your script must be at the optimum height. Test this in rehearsal: place your script high enough for you to be able to glance up without actually moving your head. As long as the script is not shielding your face, then this is the optimum position.

As with sight reading, you need to be able to read ahead if you are to feel completely confident. Look along the printed line whilst you are speaking so that you may check and be prepared for any complications which are to come, even if you have a working knowledge of the text. This method also allows you to look up from your script for quite long periods, a time you can use to consolidate communication.

8

SIGHT READING, VERSE AND PROSE

The medal examinations contain a sight reading test. Some students become very worried about this. However, if you know how to prepare for the test, that removes many of the fears.

Please read this chapter in conjunction with the previous on prepared reading and also the chapters on speaking various kinds of verse and prose.

PRACTISING SIGHT READING

Some candidates, when reading, show that they lack regular practice: they take the piece too quickly (a common fault), they become immersed in the text and forget the listener and they have trouble with individual words. Two or three minutes daily sight reading to another person is all that is required for proficiency in this art. For practice it doesn't matter what you read, a newspaper or magazine, a novel, a poem from an anthology, some junk mail which has recently come through the door all serve as grist.

When you practise sight reading make a rapid scan of the text before you start to read aloud, dealing with the following in a piece of prose:

- sort out the sense of the piece
- work phonically on any difficult words, splitting them into their sound components
- decide on the tone of the piece; know whether the material is serious or humourous, whether the text was written by an author who had his tongue in his cheek, whether the piece means more than at first appears (the author might, for example, be over-praising as a way of making a criticism), whether this is just factual information

- decide on the pace at which you feel you ought to read: this in part depends on the difficulty of the prose, on your own expertise (if you find reading difficult, then take the reading a little more slowly than you would speak a pre-learned prose excerpt, for example) and on the rate of speaking which will command the attention of the listener

If your practice piece is a poem, then look for the following:

- as with the prose, gain the overall sense of the piece and try to solve any vocabulary problems in advance

- look at the shape of the piece and try to decide what kind of poem it is: if, for example, you recognise that the poem is a sonnet, then your problems about the relation of matter to form are almost automatically solved, for you know that the writing will be contained within the two main blocks of the poem

- as with the prose, decide on the pace

REHEARSING THE READING

As you read the piece with your voice, try to read ahead with your eyes. This technique is explained in chapter seven. When you are adept at this it will help you in several ways:

- you will meet vocabulary and sense difficulties with your eyes before you have to speak any words likely to cause problems

- you will get an opportunity to puzzle out the sense before committing yourself to a spoken statement

- you will have an opportunity to raise your eyes from the text now and again and look at the listener. This helps you to make contact with him

Sight reading is more than saying words aloud. You need to read *to* someone whom you have a commitment to interest. How do you do this?

- in the first place, simply by willing to do so. If your will is in the right place, half the battle is won

- you must sort out the meaning of the text and give this meaning to the listener; use intonation changes, stresses, and any other modulatory devices which help to clarify subject matter

- you must try to be faithful to what you believe is the author's message

SIGHT READING IN THE EXAMINATION

When it is time for the sight reading test the examiner will give you an excerpt (either typed or printed) to look at. He will not expect you to read the piece immediately. Take the piece to where you are going to read it, making sure that you are in a good light, and then look carefully at the text and go through the preparatory stages that you have practised.

Most candidates prefer to read standing but there is no rule about this. If you feel the material is pleasantly relaxed and that sitting will help you convey this, then please sit down.

The examiner will tell you when he is ready to listen to your reading. Sit or stand in an advantageous position. Hold the book high enough for you merely to raise your eyes from the text, rather than move your head, when you want to make eye contact with the listener. Be careful, though, not to hide your face behind the text. The examiner may be writing notes as you read. Don't allow that to prevent you aiming to interest him for he still has his mind on your presentation. Do make sure that you are responsive to the text. If it amuses you, then smile. If the text tells of distressing events, then you must openly sympathize. When you come to the end of the reading pause for a moment, reflecting on what you have transmitted to the examiner.

Please remember to return the book to the examiner's table. Leave it open as he may wish to refer to it.

9

PERFORMING SHAKESPEARE

Bronze, Silver and Gold Medal candidates have the opportunity of taking a role from one of William Shakespeare's plays and performing an excerpt from this. Although parts of the plays are written in prose, learning to master Shakespeare's dramatic verse is an excellent training as the blend of poetry and dramatic involvement are fascinating to balance and develop. Since the plays were first written it has been possible to understand and interpret them at varying depths; the more you understand, the more authoritative and interesting can be your performance.

In this chapter I have chosen an excerpt from one of Viola's speeches in *Twelfth Night* and a speech of Lear from *King Lear*.

In writing about the teaching points which arise from the first excerpt, I have in mind the needs of a Bronze Medal candidate. The candidate will want to master:

- a background knowledge of the play
- a knowledge of the chosen role and of the other characters in the play, especially those inter-relating with the chosen role
- an understanding of dramatic verse
- the practice of bringing Shakespeare's words to life in an acting area

The choice of an excerpt from *King Lear* is aimed at a Gold Medal candidate and I have tried to demonstrate a range of approaches to Shakespeare. No one candidate is likely to attempt to study in detail each of the teaching areas I have drawn from the text but on the other hand, I hope that there is enough variety here to appeal to most performers.

The subjects I write about include:

- the themes running through the play
- roles in the play and their relationship to each other
- the original staging conditions of the play
- some ways in which actors since Shakespeare's day have thought about the selected excerpt
- ways in which the candidate may present the text
- speaking the verse

I have also made some more general remarks on performing Shakespeare and some of these may, with the guidance of the teacher, be applied to the Bronze and Silver Medal students' preparation.

Key text: *Twelfth Night*, Act II, scene ii, lines 17 – 32

Viola, disguised as a male servant to Orsino, has been accosted by Olivia's steward, Malvolio, and given a ring which he claims, incorrectly, Viola has left with his mistress.

VIOLA:

I left no ring with her: what means this lady?
Fortune forbid my outside hath not charmed her!
She made good view of me, indeed so much,
That as methought her eyes had lost her tongue,
For she did speak in starts distractedly...
 She loves me, sure – the cunning of her passion
Invites me in this churlish messenger...
None of my lord's ring! why, he sent her none...
I am the man – if it be so, as 'tis,
Poor lady, she were better love a dream...
Disguise, I see thou art a wickedness,
Wherein the pregnant enemy does much.
How easy is it for the proper-false
In women's waxen hearts to set their forms!
Alas, our frailty is the cause, not we,
For such as we are made of, such we be.

TEACHING POINTS ARISING FROM THIS TEXT

The plot and themes of *Twelfth Night*

The only way to master the plot is to read the play carefully,
making a few notes on the important happenings as you do this.
You will soon find that various characters are in love with each
other: Viola has disguised herself as a boy after being
shipwrecked and the rich countess Olivia has fallen in love
with her; for her part Viola loves Orsino, the Duke whom she
serves; Malvolio, the steward, loves Olivia who is outside his
social range; Sir Toby loves Maria (these two are well-suited
to each other) and some have noticed that Antonio the sea
captain seems to have fallen in love with Viola's twin brother
Sebastian. As well as loving other characters, some in the play
have fallen in love with themselves. Olivia, for example, tells
Malvolio that he is sick of self-love and in Olivia's assumed
grief for her dead brother and Orsino's world-weariness are
elements of self-love, too.

   Disguise also plays an important part in the play. Already
mentioned, Viola, on being wrecked on the shores of Illyria,
has put on boy's clothing as she imagines this will be a
protection for her. Feste disguises himself as a clergyman in
order to harass Malvolio. Although not fully a disguise,
Malvolio wears yellow cross-gartered hose as a sign of his
love for Olivia. Sir Andrew Aguecheek tries to assume the
character of a fighter which, too, is a change of identity.
Disguise has created all sorts of complications and gender
muddles for Viola and this excerpt presents us with her
ruminating on its dangers which she envisages as 'a
wickedness/ Wherein the pregnant enemy does much'. The
Puritans, who are mentioned several times in this play,
regarded disguise as a form of evil, and Viola seems to pick
up on this idea in the excerpt.

The role of Viola

The best way to become knowledgeable about the role of Viola
is to trace her progress through the play taking note of what

she says about herself (almost as soon as she has been washed up on the shore of Illyria she determines to search out Orsino and serve him, showing that she is as resolute as Portia in *The Merchant of Venice*) and what other people have to say about her (Olivia on first seeing Viola disguised as Cesario is instantly captured by the 'youth's perfections'). When you have collected all of this textual evidence you will have a dossier on the character you are to portray.

Interrelated roles

No character exists in a vacuum. Viola interrelates with a number of other people. You will come across most of them in compiling your notes on how Viola appears to others. Throughout much of the play her closest points of contact are with Olivia and with Duke Orsino. We see, too, how she relates to the cowardly and bullying Sir Andrew Aguecheek when he tries to pick a fight with her. At the beginning, in Sebastian's speech about his sister and at the end of the play when the twins are reunited, her relationship with her brother is made evident to the audience.

The ideas behind the excerpt

Olivia has sent her 'churlish' steward Malvolio with a ring for Viola, claiming that Viola had left it with her. Puffed up with pride, Malvolio flings the ring at Viola's feet and leaves. Instantly the girl is bright enough to realise that there is a message in the ring which the messenger had not discerned: it is a sign of Olivia's love, not for Orsino, but for Viola.

Viola begins the speech hoping that her appearance has not charmed the countess. The next five lines are a description of Olivia's behaviour during her interview with Viola. This part of the speech may possibly be spoken directly to the audience as it is purely descriptive. There is then a change in the direction of the speaking: it becomes more personal and fraught as Viola turns the address inward and speaks to her soul.

Blank verse

The verse does not rhyme and is therefore 'blank' or unrhymed, with the exception of the last couplet. When you speak the text aloud you feel that there are five stresses to each line; you use these in getting the lines to travel. By that I don't mean that you consciously bounce on each strong syllable; it is enough to feel these stresses as you speak the lines. As with any other kind of verse, where a line is not end-stopped by a punctuation mark of some sort you need to use a suspensory pause to preserve the pattern of the verse. Look for the key word in each line and work towards and then away from it. I would suggest that the really important words in the first line are 'no ring' and in the following line 'charmed'. At the end of the speech is a rhyming couplet. When you look at the complete text of the play you will see that this is not the end of the speech or the scene, which usually does end with a few lines of rhymed verse, giving a pleasing finality. Instead the couplet marks a completion of one line of Viola's thought before she starts on another idea.

You will find further advice on speaking blank verse in the teaching notes on *King Lear*.

Staging

Let us sectionalise the text:

- at the beginning of the piece Viola needs to pick up the ring; this could either be before the speaking begins or at a convenient point during the first line. If you do this whilst speaking, be careful not to interrupt the rhythm which at this juncture you are trying to establish. She also must show the audience that Malvolio has left the stage and, of course, the only practical way to do this is to follow his back with your eye focus. Perhaps Viola could stand well up-stage and watch Malvolio leave by a down-stage wing exit; the actor's face can then easily be seen

- the lines from 'She made good view of me' to 'in this churlish messenger' are a description of Olivia's behaviour during her meeting with Viola, so this section could be told directly to the audience and for that a down-stage move would be helpful

- the audience obviously needs to see Viola's face as she realises that the countess has fallen in love with her disguised form. 'I am the man' is an irony (Viola is, of course, a woman) and in speaking of Olivia loving a dream it seems to me there is evident anguish on Viola's face

- 'Disguise, I see thou art a wickedness' is almost a public condemnation. The tone again changes. There is a possibility here that Viola is going to renounce her disguise but that passes and she leads into a complicated metaphor comparing a woman's heart with a wax seal which is impressed with a signet (a man's love); the end of the excerpt is low key as Viola muses on the frailty of women; this is aptly an ironic comment as we have already seen that the heroine is a determined young woman. There are further lines in this speech but as I have cut them it would be possible for Viola to make her exit at this point. Remember, please, that in leaving, Viola's walk tells us much about her recent feelings

Throughout this piece try to convey that you are standing in a street or a public piazza in the open air. Be sure you know why you are here, what you are feeling as you speak to the audience and where you are subsequently going when you leave the stage.

A note on clothes

One has several choices in thinking about Viola's costume:

- you may like to imagine that you are performing the piece in an Elizabethan costume, in which case it will be necessary to look at several pictures of young men wearing doublet and hose and try to imagine yourself wearing these. The hose will give you plenty of freedom and in contrast the trousers and doublet are bulky and so require an open stance and large gestures

- many Shakespeare plays are performed in a costume of a later period than the Elizabethan and you may wish to adopt this practice. Draw your costume so that you have an exact idea of what it looks like and decide on the weight of the different parts of it. Today our clothes are much lighter than they were in the past

- in contrast, some presentations are given in modern dress and you may decide on that. A full costume is not envisaged in the syllabus but some candidates use token props and costume items

- in choosing what to wear make sure that the clothes help your characterization. For instance, in this selection Viola is dressed as a young man and it would be acceptable to wear a pair of trousers rather than a skirt

Key text: *King Lear*, Act III, scene iv, lines 6 – 36

Lear, Kent and the Fool are on stage; a storm is raging; Kent has brought the others to a hovel.

LEAR:

Thou think'st 'tis much that this contentious storm
Invades us to the skin: so 'tis to thee:
But where the greater malady is fixed
The lesser is scarce felt. Thou'ldst shun a bear,
But if thy flight lay toward the raging sea
Thou'ldst meet the bear i' the mouth. When the mind's free
The body's delicate: the tempest in my mind
Doth from my senses take all feeling else
Save what beats there. Filial ingratitude!
Is it not as this mouth should tear this hand
For lifting food to 't? But I will punish home.
No, I will weep no more. In such a night

To shut me out! Pour on; I will endure.
In such a night as this! O, Regan, Goneril!
Your old kind father, whose frank heart gave you all–
O, that way madness lies; let me shun that;
No more of that.

[KENT: Good my Lord, enter here.]

Prithee, go in thyself; seek thine own ease:
This tempest will not give me leave to ponder
On things would hurt me more. But I'll go in.
[*To the Fool*] In boy: go first. You houseless poverty, –

[*Exit Fool*]

Nay, get thee in. I'll pray and then I'll sleep.
Poor naked wretches, wheresoe'er you are,
That bide the pelting of this pitiless storm,
How shall your houseless heads and unfed sides,
Your looped and windowed raggedness, defend you
From seasons such as these? O, I have ta'en
Too little care of this! Take physic, pomp;
Expose thyself to feel what wretches feel,
That thou mayest shake the superflux to them
And show the heavens more just.

TEACHING POINTS ARISING FROM THE TEXT

Plot, themes and images

The intertwined themes in a Shakespeare tragedy are an intrinsic part of the play and deserve an actor's attention. In *King Lear* one theme is that of the lasting quality of kingship: can Lear simply abdicate his responsibilities as king, however elderly he may be, in order to please himself? Under his rule the kingdom had been a unity but in the hands of the Dukes of Albany and Cornwall it becomes a 'scatter'd kingdom'. Another theme is that of stripping the principal character: Lear is like an onion; each of the deprivations he suffers (kingdom, child, knights, home, sanity, clothes) is as if another skin of the onion has been peeled. One searches for the centre of the onion

– the nub of humanity in a person – wondering what it consists of. A further theme, often presented in Shakespeare's plays (*The Tempest* and *The Winter's Tale* are only two examples), is that of ingratitude within the family.

There are some key images in the play which are pursued through language and action. For example, Lear's unthroning of himself causes political disruption in the kingdom; this is obvious in the battles, whether seen or reported, during Act IV. Not so obvious is the relationship of the storm to the politics. Order on earth has been upset and, mirroring this, there is disorder in heaven, the 'late eclipses in the sun and moon' – a portent – and the tempest. The storm, too, is a psychological one, an expression of the turmoil in the mind of the aged king: Lear is much more than an old gentleman caught out in the rain, an eighteenth-century pejorative view. Other images are those of sight and blindness. Lear has been blind to the worth of his daughter Cordelia and her candour, a parallel to Gloucester who has been blind to the worth of Edgar, favouring the villainous Edmund instead. Gloucester's fault is punished with physical blinding – his eyes are gouged out – and Lear's reason – the inner sight of the mind – painfully collapses. In Tudor England the sign hanging outside a brothel was a blind-folded cupid: we have to remember that Gloucester's son Edmund is illegitimate and in the father's blinding is a suggestion that this is a punishment for adultery as well as for a lack of perspicacity.

In making these two points about theme and imagery I am trying to show that there is more than a 'story' to *King Lear*. The play works at a number of levels and you need to dig deeply to get the most from them all. Its construction is on a cosmic scale. This is more than a literary truth: I once examined a candidate who in playing Cordelia tending her deranged father forgot about scale; she presented me with a domestic miniature which might have been more at home in *Coronation Street*. To be able to bring a sense of scale to one's performance of Shakespeare is a necessary achievement.

The role and the relationships

I recommend my students to jot down every fact that they come across about the chosen character as the play is read, so that a three dimensional picture is built up about the selected role. In a Shakespeare play we learn not only by what a person does and what others say about him but also by the imagery that is used both by the character under scrutiny and also by others. This, too, is a fruitful area of study. A candidate may be tempted to present Lear merely as he appears within the limitations of the selection. If, referring to the key text, that were done, one would see only a sentimental, lonely geriatric. The examiner should be presented with the whole Lear, the man who is seen to be cruel, lecherous, inconsiderate, regal, tender, lyrical when speaking to Cordelia at the end of the play and yet terrifyingly vindictive when speaking of Goneril and Regan, wishing on them sterility so that the dynastic line becomes truncated. All these facets of Lear's humanity must lie rumbling behind the portrayal of this soaked vagabond.

It is important, too, to discover the relationships which Lear has forged with the other two characters on stage, Kent and the Fool. Kent, a generation younger than Lear, had been a member of the court; his regard for the king is stressed by his use of the eye-image (reverting to an important theme), 'let me still remain/ The true blank of thine eye.' Although banished by Lear, on hearing of the homelessness of the king, Kent had decided to seek him out. There is equal honesty but a faithfulness of another kind in the Fool's relationship with Lear: the two are so part and parcel of a single character that it has often been pointed out that Lear is the signet and the fool the obverse, the wax imprint. So these two companions are protective of Lear and something of this must come across in the way he addresses them in the excerpt.

The original staging conditions of *King Lear*

It has been conjectured that Shakespeare finished writing the play during the winter of 1604 – 5 and that it was performed at the first Globe Theatre, for which it was designed, in the season after this. The theatre was a polygonal (possibly twenty-four sided) building about 100 feet in diameter. The details of the interior have to be conjectured; a large rectangular stage jutted into the middle of the audience space, backed by a tiring house offering two entrances. An inner recess, perhaps flanked by pillars and fronted with a curtain which could be drawn aside, allowed people to enter an inner chamber, or to be discovered. Above the stage two large pillars supported a thatched roof, offering protection in wet weather.

The audience was accommodated in a series of three galleries. These ran from each side of the tiring house around the inner wall of the structure. Benches were probably provided in the galleries. Other members of the audience, the groundlings or 'penny stinkards', stood on the floor of the theatre around the thrust of the stage. An actor would have been in close contact with both the galleried people and also with those at ground level. This had a bearing on his acting style and his speaking. The large, uncluttered stage allowed for a broadness of movement and a progression up-stage would have had to be made in order to command with one's gaze the whole house. The main difference a modern performer would notice would be that acting was not a projection from the front of the stage to the audience; instead, one was aware much more of the sides of the stage which also faced a large segment of the total audience; the play had to be given to these people as well. Speech could afford to be less declaimed than in later theatres which covered a larger ground area.

Students have found it helpful to think of their own acting area as a large bare rectangle jutting into an audience. The examiner is part of that audience, now sitting where the groundlings once stood. Of course, a mental reconstruction of the Globe is not a requirement but do use your knowledge of this to help develop your own acting style and to make sense of the play text as a working document.

Studying the text

Act III is the great 'storm act' of the tragedy. Lear has been turned out of Regan's house to wander on the heath. The Fool has faithfully accompanied him and Kent has caught up with him. Half a dozen lines before the printed excerpt begins the trio had entered from the back of the stage with Kent pressing Lear to take shelter in the hovel.

In previous scenes Lear had been raging at the storm with such ferocity that by this time his energy and anger appears to have been spent. He speaks quietly to the other two characters. In spite of the foul weather he begins a highly logical tract arguing that greater dangers (the raging sea) make lesser dangers (the bear) approachable: by remaining outside in the storm Lear has his thoughts distracted from the heart-breaking ingratitude of his two daughters. In 'Save what beats there,' is an allusion to his mind: the tragic actor William Macready would strike his forehead at this point in order to emphasise the text. Gestures such as this, sparingly used, are an effective form of emphasis; repeated, they cease to have any meaning. 'Filial ingratitude', occurring immediately afterwards, is the antithesis of the reference to his mind – again, difficult to show. During these lines, until Kent makes his interjection, there is an amalgam of vindictiveness ('but I will punish home') and self-pity in the references to the stormy night. David Garrick, the eighteenth-century manager of the Theatre Royal at Drury Lane, steeped the lines with pathos, reducing his audience to tears. John Gielgud, fifty years ago in one of Granville Barker's productions, played the scene as if 'living in a distant, metaphysical world, walking and speaking strangely'. Lear's reference to himself as the 'kind father' has two meanings. There is the obvious reference to his own behaviour in comparison with that of his daughters; but there is, too, in the word 'kind' (meaning kindred or family) another reminder of the relationship of Lear to those who have expelled him. These thoughts, he realises, have the power to unbalance him completely. Making this discovery, Henry Irving rushed forward as 'a man in a dream-horror fleeing an inevitable fate'.

Shortly afterwards Lear ushers the Fool into the hovel, offering the performer another opportunity for movement as the relationship between the king and his jester are conveyed. Throughout the adversities Lear has gradually increased in thoughtfulness to the Fool and now this virtue is at its strongest.

Then occurs Lear's great prayer. It is the obverse of the curse which Lear had called down on Cordelia in the first scene of the play, not addressed to God but to the 'poor naked wretches', the many homeless in his kingdom. The imagery is complex: Lear speaks of their 'houseless heads' but then suddenly widens the house metaphor so that it applies physically to the poor people as well, seeing them as having a 'loop'd and window'd raggedness', suggesting that as the house is a protection for the body so the body is a shelter and protection for each individual soul. Entwined with all of this is Lear's penitence for his unawareness. Some writers have suggested that at this moment in the Elizabethan theatre the actor playing Lear would shift the direction of the address to the audience and to the ruling monarch if he or she were present. Many actors, Gielgud and Randal Ayrton among them, have knelt on the boards of the stage during the prayer.

The candidate has to examine this text and decide what, for him, is the climax of the piece. By including examples of how other actors played the role I've tentatively suggested several places at which the climax could occur. Having decided on the high spot of the excerpt, then the candidate must work out how the text is to be driven forward to it. Here the whole of one's technical resources come into operation: variations of dynamics, tone, pitch, the use of pauses and so on. Acting a Shakespeare scene is more than saying words: gesture and movement are also important in working towards the chosen climax.

Presenting the text

Let us think about staging this piece for examination purposes. It is important to remember that many ideas which would work in a full scale production would be unsuitable for a solo performance. Nevertheless, whatever is shown in the solo must be workable in production. You have to know the kind of theatre you would like to present the piece in and you have to understand the relationship of yourself to your imagined audience. The position of the hovel helps to anchor the text to a location and you must know where this is situated. Earlier I suggested that in the Globe this would have been at the back of the stage within the tiring house. In a solo presentation it may be inconvenient to place this up-stage because of the difficulties of working one's way there during Lear's speech. Other possible arrangements would be to position the hovel at either the right or left down-stage corners or it could be suggested by the underneath area of a table or by several chairs placed either right or left centre. Once this is established, then a simple pattern of movement may be worked out according to the way in which you wish the scene to be played.

Kent's remarks before the start of this excerpt, a repeated plea to Lear to enter the hovel, suggest that Kent is near the entrance to it but that Lear is some way away. Try to suggest that the Fool and Kent are down-stage of yourself rather than alongside you: the unsatisfactoriness of this is that you have to play in profile, directing text to the sides of the stage which looks unbecoming and dull.

Lear, from 'Thou think'st 'tis much' until 'No more of that', ignores Kent's pleas to take shelter. Instead he is buffeted by three trains of thought: there are the remarks about the tempest – both the physically wet one and also the tempest, or increasing madness, in his brain – and about filial ingratitude. The wish to punish is expressed too. Because of the turmoil within Lear it is impossible to sort the three strands out, they are interwoven and in presentation they must remain twined together.

After Kent begs Lear, for the third time, to enter the hovel, Lear obviously has to move to it and usher the Fool in; this can be a moment when he shows his genuine love and gratitude to the Fool for his care. He is about to go into the hovel himself when he suddenly wishes to pray before sleeping and chooses the open air in which to do this. Another decision is whether to pray near the opening of the hovel or to be removed from it. Furthermore, the actor must feel whether it is more right for him to kneel as the prayer is made, or whether the supplication is so wide in its compass, embracing all the homeless of the kingdom, that it is better to stand and raise one's arms in supplication like an Old Testament prophet. The last few lines of the speech (from 'Take physic, pomp') are an acting out of what circumstances have forced upon Lear and the desire to empathize with the dispossessed as he begins to shed his clothes. On that note the piece ends.

In performance one needs to give an impression of the clothes the character is wearing. It is necessary for the candidate to wear clothes which do not impede him so a formal suit would be inappropriate. I'd suggest a shirt or jumper and loosely fitting trousers. Soft shoes of some kind are another necessity. As by this time Lear's clothes are worn to ribbons by his wanderings on the heath, a long tunic of tatters could be put on over everyday clothes. If you decide not to do this, then you must imaginatively convey the raggedness of a long, heavy garment that has become stiffened with mud and soaked with rain. In this excerpt coldness and wetness are as much part of the costume as anything else.

Speaking the verse

This excerpt is an example of Shakespeare's dramatic blank verse, revealing the freedom it had acquired towards the end of his working life. You must first be aware of the underpinning rhythm and metre. Each line consists of five strong beats and (often) five unstressed syllables. The metre is grouped in iambic feet, five to the line, so that in a regular line (rare in the dramatist's later work) we would find:

/weak STRONG/ weak STRONG/ weak STRONG/ weak STRONG/ weak STRONG/

However, many of the lines are irregular and this presents problems for the speaker. To some extent these are obviated if you adopt several principles of procedure:

- listen for the five stresses in each line. Be aware of them beating inside yourself but don't vocally draw attention to them

- feel but rarely pause at the caesura which exists in the centre of each line. A punctuation mark sometimes denotes the position

The lesser is scarce felt. Thou'ldst shun a bear

but at other times you have to sense its existence. In the following line I have marked the caesura with an asterisk:

How shall your houseless heads * and unfed sides...

- discover which are the key words in each sentence. These are the main words on which the sense of the speech hangs. In the following sentences my selection of key words are capitalized

When the MIND'S free
The BODY'S delicate: the TEMPEST in my MIND
Doth from my SENSES TAKE ALL FEELING else
SAVE what beats THERE.

In this example the mental and the physical are seen as an antithesis and this has to be felt and where appropriate stressed. However, not all key words will be applied with the same stress or a relentless hammering will take place.

Notice repeated sounds. In these four lines a short 'e' recurs in such words as 'delicate', 'tempest', 'senses', 'else', 'there'. Repetition of a vowel sound (assonance) helps to convey, in this case, the fraught, nervous energy of Lear

- as with poetry, sometimes a foot in the line is reversed to give the verse impetus, or for some other reason. This can take place at the beginning of a line as in:

NO i will WEEP no MORE. in SUCH a NIGHT
to SHUT me OUT!

Rather than scribbling metrical signs above the words in your text, see if you can feel these reversals as you speak the words aloud

- make sure that the sense carries from one line to another. Even where there is an end-stopped line there must be a continuation of this or the verse is spoken in isolated pockets. Where there is no end-stopped line, as in:

How shall your houseless heads and unfed sides,
Your looped and windowed raggedness, defend you
From seasons such as these?

use a suspensory pause to tide over the sense and yet preserve the pattern of the verse line

- note the names Lear gives to people. These help to indicate the tone of his speaking. Regan and Goneril are mentioned formally by name. Not so the Fool who is fondly referred to as 'boy'. There is genuine compassion, too, in Lear's speech to the 'poor naked wretches', another naming device. So names indicate changing responses to people

- master all these technicalities in rehearsal so that when you are performing there is no need to think about them. At that time your whole concentration must be taken up with the presentation of Lear.

GENERAL CONSIDERATIONS ON PERFORMING SHAKESPEARE

Shaping the work

After you have read the complete play and decided from which scene you will present an excerpt, re-read the latter through carefully. Note its shape and try to answer such questions as:

- what is the most important moment in this scene?
- how is the action leading up to that?
- where do alternations of energy and quietness occur, if at all?
- how does the balance of power amongst the characters change, if at all?

Select your excerpt and ask much the same sort of questions about this so that you focus onto its shape, considering the climactic moment, the lead up to this, where the energy of the excerpt lies and your relationship on any given line to the characters you are addressing.

Punctuation, pause and thought

'How to act' books written fairly recently explain how characters are psychologically motivated and their authors offer advice and exercises on how to present a character with inner drives, indecisions, likings, attractions, aversions and so on. Much of this advice stems from the various writers' study of the psychologist Sigmund Freud who produced most of his works in the first three decades of this century, instructing his readers about such matters as the unconscious mind and the dominance of the will. Now Shakespeare was born long before Freud spoke of psychological motivation and so one's approach to Shakespeare's prose and verse (the latter especially) is very different than to a modern play text. One would not speak a sonnet, for example, by punctuating the lines with long pauses as one wrestled with ideas or decisions. The same holds for Shakespeare's dramatic blank verse.

Paradoxically there must be feeling and meaning in the text. How, then, is this expressed? I would suggest in the following ways:

- through the sounds of consonants and vowels as they are spoken
- through the gradations of energy with which the text is spoken
- through the imagery

The actor's basic guide is the punctuation and here he is confronted with a problem: no longer is the punctuation which Shakespeare gave his actors printed in the text you are using. Subsequent editors have introduced different and sometimes extra punctuation in order to clarify the grammatical construction of what Shakespeare had written rather than viewing the text as a blue print for performance. Helpfully, many editions (the Arden Shakespeare is one example) give notes on some of the punctuation of the First Folio, the first printed edition of all of Shakespeare's plays published in 1623, seven years after the playwright's death. Using the textual notes try to simplify the punctuation which in turn will help you to cut out unnecessary pauses in the speaking, taking the words in longer and more energetic sweeps. Remember that the pauses at full stops need to vary and some of these may be only fractional when a single thought is continued through several sentences. Other punctuation marks, the colon and the semi-colon, do not indicate that the written thought process is complete: what follows brings the idea to fulfilment.

I've already indicated that sounds can play an important part in conveying feelings, using four lines from one of Lear's speeches as an example. A couple of further examples will help to reinforce this important point.

The Tempest begins with a storm at sea. The stage represents the deck of a ship with the Boatswain in charge of operations. His commands are peppered with plosive consonants (b, d, g, p, t, k) stressing the urgency of the men in working against the storm:

> ...take in the topsail...tend to th' master's whistle

and later:

> To cabin. Silence. Trouble us not.

To convey this pressure of the moment, these sounds need to be spoken with force.

Urgency is also expressed in Miranda's first speech. She has just seen the ship go down and begs Prospero to save the drowning. Her plea is reinforced partly by plosives, used more sparingly here, and also in the nervous energy of the interjecting phrases:

> If by your art – my dearest father – you have
> Put the wild waters in this roar – allay them:
> The sky, it seems, would pour down stinking pitch,
> But that the sea, mounting to th' welkin's cheek,
> Dashes the fire out.

In the two parts of this sentence the audience has to wait, in suspense, for the completion of the interrupted sense. In turn, this suggests to the actress that speed and dynamism are required in performing these opening lines.

Use of sound cannot, of course, be a substitute for the thought processes of the character. In arriving at the major full-stops the performer has an opportunity to think as well as to establish the emotional feel of the following sentence. Strong, simple emotion can colour the words more satisfactorily than can a purely vocal approach: the latter strikes the listener as artificial, operating merely at surface level.

The imagery is, in many ways, an insight into the mind of the character, and incidentally, to that of Shakespeare. This can tell the actor and the audience as much about the character's subconscious and surface feelings as any amount of injected emotion. Again, let us look at several examples.

The first is a few lines from *Hamlet*, Act IV, scene vii, in which Queen Gertrude tells Laertes that his sister Ophelia has been drowned. In this, various trees and flowers are the images, suggesting the emotions that both Ophelia felt and that Gertrude feels as she speaks:

> There is a willow grows aslant a brook
> That shows his hoar leaves in the glassy stream;
> There with fantastic garlands did she come
> Of crow-flowers, nettles, daisies, and long purples
> That liberal shepherds give a grosser name.

If the actress playing the Queen realises that the willow tree was, in Shakespeare's day, regarded as a symbol of forsaken love, a sign that at the time of her drowning Ophelia felt that she had been jilted by Hamlet, then this guides her performance as the scene and the feelings of the character are in harmony. The same idea occurs in *Twelfth Night*, Act I, scene v, when Viola says to Olivia, 'Make me a willow cabin at your gate...'. The Queen also uses the willow as a part-picture of Ophelia floating in the brook when she mentions the hoar leaves (silvery-grey leaves) soaking in the water. When Gertrude lists the flowers, she is reliving the painful earlier scene (Act IV, scene v) in which the mad girl distributed herbs to Laertes and Claudius. The symbolism of the flowers refers to both Ophelia and Gertrude: the crow-flowers were given the country name 'fair maids of France' and the derivation of daisy is 'day's eye', the dawning of the day, a symbol of Ophelia's young life. On the other hand the 'grosser name' by which long-purples were known was 'the rampant widow', a just description of Gertrude. The actress preparing this speech can profitably consider Gertrude's reaction to this uncomplimentary symbol.

For the second example of imagery as a revelation of the character's mind we shall turn again to *The Tempest* with its ideas of the sea, of storms, of drowned men and of a wild island. Let us study Francisco's description of the fight of

Ferdinand – the heroic young prince who ultimately gains the hand of Miranda – against the sea when his ship foundered. It occurs in Act II, scene i:

> I saw him beat the surges under him
> And ride upon their backs; he trod the water,
> Whose enmity he flung aside, and breasted
> The surge most swoln that met him: his bold head
> 'Bove the contentious waves he kept, and oared
> Himself with his good arms in lusty stroke
> To th' shore, that o'er his wave-worn basis bowed,
> As stooping to relieve him...

All of the imagery suggests that Francisco, one of the lords of Milan, admires Ferdinand: his first image is of the young man riding on the backs of the waves, as if they were horses; he then points to the sea as the 'enemy', and likewise uses the word 'contentious' (meaning 'quarrelsome') as an adjective to describe the waves; he compares Ferdinand's arms making for the shore with a rower's oars. The images not only show us what a fine fellow Ferdinand is, but they also reiterate the theme that nature on and around Prospero's isle is basically hostile to man. Notice that the whole speech is contained within a sentence suggesting that there is great drive in the speaking with the result that any breath taken is snatched quickly at the semi-colons.

The stress on words

What I have written about metrical stress when dealing with one of Shakespeare's sonnets holds good when looking at dramatic blank verse. Briefly, one has to select the key words, as I've demonstrated in the *King Lear* passage, and ensure that these receive a stress. Remember that a key word frequently occurs near the end of a line, to which your voice must attain. Avoid stressing unimportant words. 'And' often gains prominence: avoid any emphasis on conjunctions such as 'and', 'but' and 'so'. There is no need to stress or colour adjectives and adverbs for the important word is the noun or verb they qualify. Similarly pronouns are often unimportant words unless there is an 'I/thou' antithesis.

Movement

Occasionally a candidate reduces to a recitation a Shakespeare speech by robbing it of movement and emotion. Both are needed. Make sure that movement is appropriate to character and situation. Sometimes I've watched Helena and Hermia in *A Midsummer Night's Dream* performing with very little movement at a time when the text suggests that they are clambering through the forest.

Movement and emotion must be commensurate. If you are performing a character who is over-wrought or making vengeful curses on those who have wronged him, then your movement, as well as your speaking, must show this agitation by the rapidity of both speech and walk. The rate of one's movement is linked to that of the speaking.

Movement must also indicate the costume the performer is wearing. If you have decided that your character is dressed in Elizabethan clothes then look at paintings and drawings of people of Shakespeare's period – those of Holbein, for example – to gain an impression of the bulk of costumes. Often the shape of the dress is determined by what is worn beneath the top layer and to find information about this you must go to illustrated books on costume or to costume collections such as the one in the Victoria and Albert Museum in London or the collection in Bath. Today most of our clothes are fairly light; not so in Elizabethan times. Therefore give an impression not only of the bulk but also of the weight of period clothes. This applies especially to roles in which a court dress or state and ceremonial robes are worn. In consequence one's carriage must be erect with shoulders as wide as possible to suggest the outline of the wearer. Gestures, too, by their broadness help to convey the massiveness of sleeves and cuffs.

In addition to his carriage, the player of Shakespeare must adopt the right kind of stance to show costume to its fullest effect. A common characteristic of paintings of young men and women is that the subject uses as much of the personal space around himself as he can, whether he is standing or sitting. This helps to make an impression on the beholder.

Similar considerations would hold if you had decided to set your chosen play in a later historic period. Sometimes, of course, it is appropriate to present a Shakespeare play in modern dress, provided the difficult task of matching Elizabethan verse with contemporary costume had been achieved without a hint of disjointedness.

The theatre envisaged

No stipulation is made in the syllabus about the kind of theatre you are to envisage when you perform your Shakespeare selection. You could decide that, most directly, you are giving a performance to a small group of people sitting in the examination room. The audience might be arranged in a block in front of you or it could be spread on three sides around the edge of the room. Whatever, it is important that you are aware of the position of the audience and send part of the text to it as the direction of Elizabethan acting was rarely restricted to the stage area. Remember that the examiner thinks of himself as a part of the envisaged audience; he is neither an isolated person to whom much of a speech must be addressed nor someone to be ignored. Please don't use the examiner as a character in the excerpt to whom you are talking, nor people the area behind him with imaginary supers.

An alternative to thinking of the examination room as your theatre is to imagine that you are on a modern stage. In this case, temper the presentation so that it is suitable for the room; the examination is not a test of rant and roar. On the other hand projection is important: words, meaning and character must come across with dynamic assurance. Judge what is appropriate!

Earlier in this chapter I gave you some notes on the Elizabethan playhouse. This could well be the place of performance for candidates with a historical interest. It is important to consider the actor-audience relationship and, if required, the position of entrances and exits.

It is helpful to the examiner if you explain the theatrical context you have in mind when you introduce the piece.

Beginning and ending

Sometimes I find that the beginnings and endings of presentations are ragged and spoil a good performance.

Before starting your presentation make sure that the acting area is as you need it. Any superfluous furniture should be put to one side of the room. Avoid leaving unwanted chairs at the back of the playing area as they are a distraction. Quickly, but accurately, set any furniture that you need. Once your stage is prepared, announce your piece and as part of this introduction give a note on the kind of theatre you envisage playing in. If need be, indicate where imagined characters are placed but normally your performance should make this evident. Don't rush straight into the speaking. Spend a quiet moment in assuming the role within its intellectual and emotional setting. Some actors like to do this turned away from the examiner but there is no convention to follow. Then perform!

At the end of the excerpt I have frequently seen candidates leap out of the role much too quickly. Finish with a tableau held for a couple of seconds and then adopt neutrality.

FOR FURTHER READING

Adams, J C, *The Globe Playhouse* (1961)

Barton, L, *Historic Costume for the Stage* (1961)

Berry, C, *The Actor and the Text* (revised edition, 1993)

Brockbank, Philip, *Players of Shakespeare I* (1989)

Brown, John Russell, *Shakespeare's Plays in Performance* (1969)

Clemen, Wolfgang, *The Development of Shakespeare's Imagery* (1951)

Clemen, Wolfgang, *Shakespeare's Soliloquies* (1987)

Cox, Brian, *The Lear Diaries: the Story of the Royal National Theatre's productions of Shakespeare's Richard III and King Lear* (1992)

Crowl, Samuel, *Shakespeare Observed: studies in Performance on Stage and Screen* (1992)

David, Richard, *Shakespeare in the Theatre* (1978)

Edwards, C, ed, *The London Theatre Guide, 1576–1642* (1979)

Gurr, Andrew, *Studying Shakespeare* (1988)

Harrison, G B, *Introducing Shakespeare* (1954)

Hodges, C Walter, *Shakespeare's Second Globe* (1973)

Holt, Robin J, *Scenes from Shakespeare: a Notebook for Actors* (1988)

Jackson, Russell and Smallwood, Robert, *Players of Shakespeare II* (1988)

Joseph, B L, *Elizabethan Acting* (1951)

Laver, James, *A Concise History of Costume* (1969)

Leech, C and Craik, T W, *The Revels History of Drama in English, vol iii, 1576–1613* (1975)

Linklater, Kristin, *Freeing Shakespeare's Voice: the Actor's Guide to Talking the Text* (1992)

Loney, Glenn, *Staging Shakespeare: Seminars on Production Problems* (1990)

Lusardi, James P, *Reading Shakespeare in Performance: King Lear* (1991)

Nagler, A M, *Shakespeare's Stage* (1981)

Salgado, G, *King Lear (Text and Performance)* (1984)

Spencer, T B, *Shakespeare: A Celebration* (1964)

Teague, Francis N, *Shakespeare's Speaking Properties* (1991)

Tillyard, E M W, *The Elizabethan World Picture* (1943)

Wells, Stanley, ed, *The Cambridge Companion to Shakespeare Studies* (1986)

Film

Twelfth Night, directed by Trevor Nunn (1996)

Elizabethan Style Theatres

A couple of Elizabethan style theatres exist and it is an instructive experience to see one of Shakespeare's plays performed in this setting. The reconstruction of the Globe Theatre is complete on Bankside, Southwark. The complex also contains a highly informative museum. The Maddermarket Theatre in Norwich is a further example. Although not slavishly mirroring the layout of an Elizabethan theatre, the Swan at Stratford-upon-Avon provides a thrust stage and galleries which the actors of the Royal Shakespeare Company use imaginatively.

10

SOLO ACTING

This chapter is written with candidates for the Associate Recital Diploma in mind. It should be read in conjunction with the previous, even if a non-Shakespeare selection is chosen, as many of the points dealt with at length there are only summarised here.

THE CHOICE

The choice of excerpt would depend on several factors:

- if a theme has been chosen, then the selected passage could introduce a variation on this

- the choice is an opportunity to demonstrate the candidate's technical accomplishment in acting a scene from a play

- the selected excerpt may be a contrast in subject and style compared with the other pieces performed

Avoid selecting from an anthology of audition pieces. It is important that the complete play is studied, for the presentation of the excerpt must be truthful to the overall intention of the playwright and the tone of the drama.

Make sure that the excerpt is suitable for solo performance. Sometimes candidates choose part of a play which depends for its effect on the cut and thrust of a conversation. However skilful the performer is at suggesting the presence of a further person, the impact of the dialogue is vitiated when half of it is left unspoken.

THE SELECTED ROLE

The role, too, must be related to the whole play. Sometimes the chosen character is presented as he exists only in the selected episode, bearing no relation to the developed conception revealed in the complete work. On reading the play it is important to jot down all the salient facts about the character. These can then be ploughed into the presentation with the result that a fully rounded person is discovered.

Additionally the character must be true to the conventions of the period. For example, from the Restoration until the end of the Georgian period a popular convention held that a country girl, having married an urban gentleman and settled in London, adjusted in speech and behaviour to metropolitan society with remarkable rapidity. Lady Teazle (*The School for Scandal*) is an exponent of this practice and the convention was accentuated in Richard Sheridan's choice of Frances Abington, a polished actress who moved in aristocratic circles, to play the part in his comedy. It was only at the end of the eighteenth century when this tradition was passing into abeyance that Dorothy Jordan played the role with a rural enthusiasm. The practice was established as early as 1675 when William Wycherley created Marjorie Pinchwife (*The Country Wife*), a young woman of charm and rectitude, brought by her husband to London and presented in society to great acclaim. On stage I have seen her degraded to a rustic buffoon in a misplaced attempt at comedy acting.

Having studied the selected role, you must then make that character belong to you. There are several ways of doing this. Some actors enjoy finding an actual person who approximates to the role in order to make a study of that individual as discreetly as possible. A small notebook to enter details can be very useful. Much of what you observe may then be incorporated into the characterisation. Or you may observe a number of people, taking various traits such as their ways of thinking, physical idiosyncrasies, speech patterns, and so on, and merge consistent elements together so that a character is gradually built up from these.

Instead of observation an actor sometimes digs inside his own experiences of life and tries to discover through these how the character would react to the various situations outlined in the text. Whilst the observation method of building a character consists of the application of a number of externals, in this method you are engaged in an interior exploration.

Once you begin to appreciate how your character 'works', try living part of your life as that person: take on the role as you shave in the morning or buy a newspaper or walk down the road. However inventive you are in the characterization be careful that this creation is truly human and not just a bundle of cyphers. Everything – speech, movement, gesture and thought – must spring from a human heart. If you fail in that, then the character fails and you are left with nothing more than a dangling puppet.

In the previous chapter much space was spent in considering the voice of the actor in performance and so here I make only a few remarks on this subject. Sometimes performers try to use a voice which is not their own in order to present the character. The consequence is that the speaking becomes uninteresting as the false voice limits the modulatory range. Whatever you are attempting, dialect, aging, fear and so on, must spring from your own natural voice.

Do make sure that you know your lines thoroughly. The characterization must be presented with authority and this is wanting if your mind is set on recall instead of on the thoughts and emotions of the character. Examination conditions present their own distractions and these can easily drive words from one's head. Try setting up a counter-irritant when you think you know your lines: say them with the radio playing at full blast. This soon reveals any areas where there is an uncertainty in the learning.

Your presentation, as well as introducing a chosen character to an audience, is also a study in relationships. How does your chosen character relate to the 'other' people you are creating on the stage through your artistry? So much informs the audience about this: there is body language as well as the spaces between yourself and the imagined character. If you keep yourself removed from this person, then your relationship appears distant and unfriendly but if you are able to come close to each other, or hold hands or make physical contact in some other way, then fondness, care or love are apparent. The way in which we look at another person also tells an onlooker much about a relationship: this is to do with eye focus, with the angle at which one's head is held as you regard a person, the amount of eye contact you chose to make or, of course, the absence of this which can suggest that you are uneasy in the presence of the other.

The physical portrayal of a character is greatly helped by several items of costume such as a practice skirt, a hat or character-assisting footwear. These must be suitable for the character as drawn by the playwright. I once saw Gwendolen (*The Importance of Being Earnest*) played by a candidate carrying a man's battered black umbrella and wearing a pair of Dr Marten's remarkably sturdy lace-up boots. Everything about this candidate's presentation of herself negated Oscar Wilde's creation. The decision about footwear is important. Beryl Reid once said that character begins with what the actress has on her feet. I am unhappy when I find candidates of both sexes playing Shakespeare in bare feet: they claim this gives them greater freedom – suitable in the case of personating Ariel or Puck – but why would this apply to Hamlet or Macbeth?

Period deportment and its effect on gesture and movement is part of the portrayal. If a full period costume is not used, then the candidate must imaginatively convey this through the use of his body. Women candidates can easily forget the influence on overall shape and movement of heavy and restrictive underwear. Similarly the bulk and weight of a woman's dress is also to be noted.

Suitable props can also help the characterization. These should all be of the same period (a quill pen and a sheet of file paper are a peculiar incongruity) and an 'all-or-nothing' principle holds: you cannot wield a teapot but not use cups and saucers.

ORGANISING THE STAGE

Try to keep furniture and props to the minimum. Dealing with these can cause an unwelcome hold-up to the flow of the recital and so damage the pace which may have built up by the time the dramatic excerpt is presented. As part of your usual rehearsals, place the furniture that is to be used in performance so that you are accustomed to making decisions about its disposition. The room in which you give your presentation may well be larger than that in which you rehearse. Don't be tempted to play over too large an area: should you do this you easily become rushed because of overmuch travel; you might also lose pace. A performance kept within limited bounds gains in strength. Have in mind a rectangle of pre-determined dimensions and keep the acting within that.

Candidates often use an empty chair to indicate the presence of a person. Question whether this is desirable. The chair may simply reveal that it is empty; with your eye-focus and direction of playing you should be able to convey the reality of 'the other person' more adequately.

In planning the movement pattern of the scene try to keep yourself upstage of any imagined characters. You are then able to direct your remarks downstage to the unseen presences and so out to the audience. Sometimes in an examination recital the imagined character stays remarkably still for a long while. A most effective lift is given to the scene if, through the turn of your gaze and your change of eye-focus, you suggest that the character has moved. Some performers place the imagined person they are playing against too near the side of the acting area. The effect is that much of the speaking is directed to the wings, or worse, to the side wall of the room. It is often preferable to place *yourself* near the wings for a while and direct your remarks centrally downstage.

If you are the only person on the stage be careful about the direction of your playing and the conventions current at the time of the first performance of the drama you have selected. In Restoration and Georgian pieces the audience played a part in each performance to the extent that the house could count as another performer. Much of the dialogue of plays of these periods must be directed outwards to the auditorium and to the side boxes as well as to other characters on the stage. Later, with their presentations of naturalistic drama at the Prince of Wales' Theatre, Squire and Marie Bancroft created drawing rooms in which real families could live (a distinguished visitor grumbled to Bancroft that the settings made him dissatisfied with the decor of his own home) and a pretence was made that the proscenium opening was covered by a fourth wall. In playing excerpts from Tom Robertson's or Oscar Wilde's dramas it would be inappropriate for a solo performer to attempt to talk through the fourth wall at the audience. Instead, a monologue must be regarded as the character voicing his thoughts to himself.

MOVES

Key work: *The Maids* by Jean Genet

Judiciously planned moves can helpfully divide the text into its component parts. The thought process lying behind the words indicates when a move could be made. Consider this speech of Claire in *The Maids* by Jean Genet:

> We've read the story of Sister Holy Cross of the Blessed Valley who poisoned twenty-seven Arabs. She walked without shoes with her feet all stiff. She was lifted up, carried off to the crime. We've read the story of Princess Albanarez who caused the death of her lover and her husband. She uncorked the bottle and made a big sign of the cross over the goblet. As she stood before the corpses, she saw only death and, off in the distance, the fleeting image of herself being carried by the wind. She made all the gestures of earthly despair. In the book about the Marquise de Venosa, the one who poisoned her children, we're told that, as she approached the bed, her arms were supported by the ghost of her lover.

I'll be supported by the sturdy arms of the milkman. I'll lean my left hand on the back of his neck. He won't flinch. You'll help me. And, far away, Solange, if we have to go far away, if I have to leave for Devil's Island, you'll come with me. You'll board the boat. The flight you were planning for him can be used for me. We shall be that eternal couple, Solange, the two of us, the eternal couple of the criminal and the saint. We'll be saved, Solange, saved, I swear to you!

(*She falls on Madame's bed*)

There is much about poison in *The Maids*: Claire and Solange, who are continually performing the roles of maid and mistress in turn, plan to poison their madame. The plan misfires and in a strange ritual Claire assumes the character of the mistress and drinks the poisoned tea, savouring each sip whilst Solange speaks a bare poem about role change and death. The setting of this short play is Madame's over-decorated Louis Quinze bedroom.

The purpose of looking at the excerpt is to see how movement might sectionalize text and bring out the ideas latent in the subtext. Claire has been talking to Solange about killing Madame, asking for her help with this. The two locational reference points are the bed and the stool at the dressing table.

A possibility would be to place Solange against the pillows at the head of the bed. Claire is standing on the floor, looking at Solange, in a state of ecstasy. Three poisonings are mentioned and it would be appropriate if between each there were a move so that the bed became part circled. Genet often seems to be fascinated by church ritual and this could be almost a liturgical procession. The tone of the speaking changes in the second paragraph. The pseudo-hagiographic writing has ended: this is no longer a procession in honour of perverted 'saints' but rather a play Claire acts for the benefit of Solange about the embrace with the milkman. Some of this might well be taken sitting in front of the dressing-table facing Solange. Very rapidly the play changes into another ritual, this time of self-dramatisation in which Claire involves Solange. By the time she gets to the last sentence Claire is standing, ecstatic as she lunges across the room to the bed on which, according to the direction, she flings herself. I have suggested that there are five basic moves within this text. It is advisable to keep the pattern of movement simple in a solo presentation.

When you are not making a move, plant both feet on the ground and be still or sit and be still. Before the move, inhale and then travel on an outgoing breath. Know exactly where you are to get to and then, again, stand still, feet firmly on the floor. Tension and excitement in one's speaking produce tense and excited moves.

Before leaving the business of movement, a word of caution: some candidates rely on an acting edition of the play and slavishly follow the moves given in this. What works well in a full scale production of a play is almost inevitably doomed to failure when transposed to a solo performance. Furthermore the directions given in acting editions refer to the physical set-up of the West End theatre in which the play was first staged: this bears no comparison with the simplicity of the examination room. You have to work out your own pattern of movement which will suit both an empty space and a solo performer and yet still be true to the intention of the playwright.

THREE QUESTIONS

In the course of your preparation, before you start to rehearse the piece, I'd suggest you ask yourself three questions:

- Where am I? Have a clear impression of the setting in which you are playing. Think of the ways in which you relate to this setting

- Why am I about to go on stage? There must be a purpose in your entry, or if you are already on stage, for your presence there. Know why you are appearing in the location

- What frame of mind am I in? Your mental attitude affects thought, speech and movement and so to be completely familiar with this is an important influence on your acting

- At the examination, before you begin your dramatic excerpt, mentally run through the answers to these questions. They will anchor your performance

INTRODUCING THE EXCERPT

Introduce the play title and the author. If the play is well known (take it that all of Shakespeare's are) there is no need to give further information. Otherwise a brief note on the character you play is useful to the examiners. Avoid giving a plot summary. Set your stage before you introduce the play. In this way the announcement is an immediate prelude to the performance.

FURTHER READING

Barkworth, Peter, *The Complete About Acting* (1991)
Briggs, Julia, *This Stage-Play World* (1983)
Christoffersen, Eric Exe, *The Actor's Way* (1993)
Desberg, Peter and Marsh, George D, *Controlling Stage Fright* (1988)
Harrop, John, *Acting* (1992)
Hayman, Ronald, *How To Read A Play* (1977)
Martin, Jacquelin, *Voice In Modern Theatre* (1991)
Olivier, Laurence, *On Acting* (1986)
Shiach, Don, *From Page To Performance* (1987)
Young, Jordan R, *Acting Solo* (1989)

11

PLANNING A PROGRAMME FOR MEDAL EXAMINATIONS

I've left considerations of the choice of pieces until near the end of this book as I find it more workable to study a range of possibilities and then, having raised several to performance standard, to make the selection. It is very difficult to know if a piece 'fits' you until you have worked on it. Study also stands you in good stead in the discussions. It is much better to discover literature itself through performing, wherein you get a first hand acquaintance with a book or poem, than by reading about it in potted histories.

Candidates in the medal examinations present an excerpt from a Shakespeare play and either a prose excerpt or a poem from the lists in the syllabus; the choice is constrained by the syllabus. Having said that, however, I've noticed that some candidates make much wiser choices than others. Factors which influence the choice of material are:

- the suitability of a piece for the individual abilities of a particular candidate
- the contrast between the prose or verse and the selected Shakespeare
- the contrasting periods of the selected pieces
- the unity existing between the pieces

THE INDIVIDUAL CANDIDATE

The Shakespeare role must be suitable for the particular abilities of the candidate. I have, for example, seen both Puck and Ariel played by earth-bound performers when the characteristics of the roles demand a nimbleness and the impression that at any minute these beings have the propensity to fly away. Candidates need to be able to recognise their strengths (examiners often point these out in their reports) and choose a role accordingly.

The age of the candidate is another important factor especially in the Shakespeare selection. There is a tradition in the theatre that mature actresses may play Juliet and Hamlet is often portrayed by a man well towards middle-age. The reason frequently proffered for this is that only a mature and experienced performer is able to unravel the complexity of roles such as these. This might be true: but there is a difference between an older person playing Juliet in the theatre with the kindly disguises of costume, make-up and sympathetic lighting and performing this in the unadorned world of the examination room. So my advice to older candidates is to think of your age as a help in eliminating unsuitable roles.

CONTRASTS

During the time of preparation the candidate studies the effect of juxtaposing one piece against another: the contrast between the dramatic selection and the non-dramatic work might be exploited. One might chose a lyrical speech of Rosalind (*As You Like It*) and then consider from the listed selections a piece contrasting in spirit, a violent episode from a novel perhaps. Characters, too, offer contrasts. One might develop a theme by taking a Shakespeare character – say the Porter in *Macbeth* – and compare him with a contrasting portrait from the lists of stipulated pieces.

UNITY

Contrast is not the only principle on which one may work: there is also that of unity. In this we discover ways in which one piece reflects some of the ideas in the other. An example would be to use the Shakespeare excerpt suggested in Chapter 9 (King Lear in the storm) and to take a piece of verse or prose from the lists of stipulated pieces in which a character in need or despair is considered from a different viewpoint.

I have written further about the selection of poetry and prose pieces in chapters 1, 2 and 6.

BACK TO PERFORMANCE

I began this book by writing about style in performance. Let me follow this up by mentioning several technicalities which will help to give your recital a degree of polish.

Decide in advance on the order of your pieces. I am amazed how often, when I ask about the order, a candidate laconically says, 'It doesn't matter!' It does!! It is a workable principle to progress from the piece demanding least energy to the most. For example, it is good to 'try out' the room on a poem or a prose piece and then go on to the dramatic. Some Shakespeare excerpts are highly charged with emotion and if you know the soundings of the room or hall there is less chance of over-projecting and so putting on a performance which is empty blast and lacking in strong feeling. You may work on other principles; that is fine as long as you try the order in rehearsal and judge what makes for the most satisfactory presentation.

When you come into the examination room remember that for a successful performance you are in charge. Firstly, you must be confident. If you find several opportunities before the examination to present your recital to others, that is a great advantage. It may be possible to arrange this at school or at a club to which you belong. Be on the look out for opportunities and don't hesitate to offer your work to voluntary organisations or to institutions such as a home for old people who would enjoy meeting you and several other candidates for a short entertainment one afternoon.

Before you leave for the examination make sure that you have everything you need. Put materials ready the day before, including any props you have rehearsed with for the Shakespeare selection. Make sure your examination copies are to hand and please put scripts in the order of presentation.

When you go into the examination room, whilst the examiner is making introductory notes about your pieces, have a quick look around the room and decide how best to employ the space. Get any furniture ready for the whole recital rather than breaking into it midway with a shifting of tables and chairs.

As the pieces are restricted to those in the syllabus and the examiner will know them, there is no need to make more of your introduction than the titles. A sentence about the staging of the dramatic excerpt may make your intentions clearer: are you envisaging performing in an Elizabethan theatre or for the space in which you find yourself? does the disposition of other characters need comment? is your conception of the production radical in any way? In any of these cases a word at the beginning would help the examiner to understand what is happening.

When the time comes the examiner will tell you whether or not he wants a short break between the pieces to note anything on your report. If he does, then quietly sit and relax until he indicates that he wants you to resume.

Some examiners write through the latter part of each piece. Don't let this distract you in any way. Carry on with your performance as you have always given it. Much more is seen and heard than you suspect.

At the end of each piece wait in a recollective tableau for a few seconds and then relax.

These few pointers will, I hope, help you to give a recital of quality. In the course of a day an examiner sees many people and he is cheered by those who are friendly and approachable. They have learnt – and it is a point everyone should bear in mind – that the examiner wants the candidate to succeed. At the same time he has to preserve the standards which the Academy has set over the years.

MARKS AND REMARKS

Some candidates put too great a store on marks and neglect the remarks made on the report form. The marks show in a comparative way your present standard in the areas stipulated on the report (Voice, Diction, etc.). They are a good indication of where you are successful or show promise and of those areas where you need to raise the standard. Sometimes the written remarks form an amplification of this. At other times further points to be made about your work are brought by the examiner to your attention.

Finally, enjoy all of your work. The preparation and the performance go hand in hand together and both help to increase your enthusiasm for the presentation of prose and poetry.

12

PLANNING FOR THE ASSOCIATE RECITAL DIPLOMA EXAMINATION

THE REQUIREMENTS

The syllabus expresses either openly or by implication the anticipations of the two examiners who form the audience for the Diploma Recital. These may be summarised as follows:

- the candidate is going to present six different works to the examiners and through his performance he is going to show his mastery of various literary forms. The diploma is the culmination of a progression of grade and medal examinations in verse and prose and one may assume that all of the skills and artistic demands of these are going to serve the presentation

- this means that the candidate must have a sound understanding of the various literary forms he will use as well as of the various writers' aims and their place in the history of literature and ideas

- this is a marriage of practical performance and appreciation

- there is to be nothing dry about the recital. It is not an academic exercise, it is an entertainment. As such it must sparkle and throughout delight the audience. Within the bounds of a successful recital various supports may be used to enhance the work and these will be dealt with later in this chapter

- the candidate will present a balanced programme. The requirements outlined in the syllabus are helpful in achieving this and the time limit ensures that the recital is compact. Balance, however, does not mean that the candidate's personal interests have to be sacrificed

- here is an opportunity to construct a programme around pieces which appeal to you and challenge your abilities

CLUSTERS

The syllabus requires the pieces to be centred on a theme. There are several ways of working towards a theme. One may begin by rehearsing pieces known for a long while, probably outstripping the half dozen forms itemised in the syllabus, and then asking yourself why you like this cluster. This is almost a *Desert Island Discs* approach. Once you begin to answer the question, you may find that certain ideas are common to the pieces. They can then be related to events in your life or to your developing tastes.

On the other hand you may wish to begin by constructing some sort of parameter in the shape of a subject or theme to your choice and there is nothing wrong with this provided that you are prepared to extend the fences or even to knock them down altogether if occasion demands. At the start it is important to say that the theme must be something to which you have a strong commitment. Don't be conventional (avoid 'The Seasons' and any other bland titles loved by poetry anthology compilers) or overtly literary, unless reading and writing plays a great part in your life.

As I write I remember pictures that I have seen over the past few weeks on the television which have left a deep and lasting impression on me. Some of these could easily be titled with such tags as 'Homelessness', 'Children in Need', 'The Pain of War', 'Old Age' and, provided personal commitment was there, could begin to spark off a collection of pieces for a programme. Some candidates may adopt a historical approach: 'Taking the Waters' suggests the rise of the British spa and a quizzical look at its frequenters. 'An Actor's Life for Me' could reflect the life of travelling performers in the eighteenth century as is shown zestfully in John O'Keeffe's play *Wild Oats*. Both the first and second world wars produced their own writers: the well-known poets of the first world war, the many plays which tell of the courage of ordinary people in the second world war, and in a different genre the inspired speeches of Sir Winston Churchill: all this is matter for an anthology. For some, the candidate's home town may suggest material. Oxford, where I live, has been described in poetry and prose by such writers as John Henry Newman, Gerard Manley Hopkins, Matthew Arnold, Max Beerbohm and Compton Mackenzie as well as by the vast number of eventual writers who studied at its colleges and the tourists with their correspondence and journals describing the place. Sometimes it is the small, now forgotten, place which has drawn writers to it. Netley Abbey, a ruined Cistercian monastery on the banks of Southampton Water, serves as an example. It was visited by many late eighteenth and early nineteenth century poets who used it as a subject for moon-lit verses as well as by Richard Wilson who wrote a horror-story about the place and Isaac Pocock who used it as the setting for a musical play, each taking the name of the abbey for a title. More to the centre of things is the district around the British Museum, Bloomsbury, which drew to itself a band of writers and artists and so these again provide plenty of material by virtue of living within close proximity of each other.

Try not to fix on the subject of the recital or the finalization of the selection too quickly. Experiment with a wide range of pieces within the various categories and see what you are happy with. This is not a waste of time as by tackling a range you will be getting your appreciative and vocal faculties in training. But, of course, you will eventually construct the recital and then you are ready to consider the introduction and the linking remarks.

The introduction is an opportunity to share with the audience the reasons for grouping together the six selections and commenting on the inclusion of various works.

You must decide what kind of links are suitable for your presentation. You may wish to say a few words about the writer of each piece and place the work in some kind of literary and biographical context. Or the theme could be of greater importance and so you talk about that, seeing how different writers at various periods have made their response to your subject. If your selection is from a single author, then you may want to relate the various pieces to his development as a writer and the events of his life which helped to shape his work. I'd suggest that you don't learn by heart the link passages, even though you may feel more secure in doing so. Much is said by rote in the recital and spontaneous speech with its natural hesitations and informality of expression gives the listener a different sound texture.

In planning the recital, try to keep in mind an overall picture of it. It is more than a series of contrasts. Just as in an individual piece you look for the climax of the writing, so in the recital you need a text towards which you drive the whole performance. As you ponder over possibilities and running order ask yourself from time to time, 'Where is this leading?'. When you have decided that, make sure that you are taking the audience with you on this journey.

WHEREIN IS QUALITY?

You will understand that as you are attempting to gain a diploma there must be a recognisable quality about your work. Wherein does this quality lie?

The previous section suggests that you need to be a person who enjoys a wide range of literature and can build up an entertaining and thoughtful programme with this. You must be skilful, too, in shaping the programme. You must know not only what you want to give your audience but also what you want the audience to get from the recital. When you have gone from the room, something of your performance must remain with the examiners.

One of the really important qualities you need to possess is vocal range and technique. Younger students often ignore this and are unwilling to undertake regular voice exercises without which the vocal range is limited and unresponsive. Some candidates even labour under the misapprehension that the acquisition of a vocal technique destroys the performer's sincerity. A mastery of vocal technique will release your voice so that you may convey your sincerity unimpeded.

Allied to this is the need to master the speaking of a number of literary forms. The early chapters in this book take each of these forms, considering them in some detail. Do therefore make sure that you are thoroughly conversant with the form itself and can see the way in which material content relates to it.

But there is more to the recital than text and voice. You are a visible person: you must therefore have stage presence. From the moment you walk into the examination room you must be a performer in whom the audience has confidence; you must be an authority on the material you are to present and that authority must assert itself through your whole personality. Your physical presence contributes considerably to the recital. Therefore think very carefully about what you wear, when and where you stand or sit, the part that movement plays in the recital as a whole and the way in which your body amplifies and underlines what you say. These subjects have been covered in previous chapters.

AIDS TO PRESENTATION

There are many aids which can help you. Just a few of these are considered here. Please bear in mind that you must select what is appropriate for your programme and for yourself.

However flexible your voice, there are times when a change from it is a welcome interlude. Here music can play its part. Most direct is the ability to play an instrument; a guitar, for example, neither impedes the flow of your recital nor becomes a barrier between you and your audience. Your playing needs to be of a high standard in order to maintain the professionalism of the performance. Failing this, a tape recorder may be used with discretion and also unobtrusively, which means practice in manipulation. One elderly candidate I met used her understanding of dance as a link between several of the pieces and this was a pleasant way of giving a lift to the recital.

I have seen slides used to great effect during recitals. Again, this means that a technical mastery of the apparatus is essential. Slides could be used either between pieces, provided the pace did not slacken, or, with discernment, as the speaking takes place. If the latter, then an automatic change device is required as the speaker should devote the whole of his attention to communicating the written word.

Simple props may play a part. I saw an expressionless half-mask used to great effect during an excerpt from a Greek play. It was as if an extra person had joined the candidate. Another candidate produced from a property basket a pair of puppet heads on poles and used these for a ballad which depended on two voices.

The dress of the candidate is of the greatest importance and this is where women score over men: it is a matter of imaginativeness. When I was a child women folk singers sometimes visited our school in one of the Welsh valleys wearing a dress with wide sleeves and a train, transforming the wearer into a variety of characters. Something of the sort could be of great use to women candidates in their recital.

FURNITURE

There will be chairs in the examination room for you to use and there will probably be a table available. One of the examination pieces must be read: are you going to hold the text or use a lectern? I've found my own light-weight portable lectern very helpful in giving recitals as I'm used to having my text at a certain height and the lectern ensures that this happens. Whether held or placed on something, it is advantageous to put the pages in a hard-back folder; not only does this look more tidy, the folder is useful in preventing the pages limply falling over.

PLANNING THE STAGE MANAGEMENT

Some candidates seem surprised that there is a stage management side to the recital. You may however be using simple token costumes, musical apparatus, slides and props. Hopefully you will change your position in the performance area a number of times so that visual variety is obtained. All of this has to be very carefully thought out so that your recital flows without interruption. Always make sure that a movement ends near to the next piece of apparatus that you require. Whatever changes take place in the course of the recital they must be an interesting and tidy part of the total show. I have seen a person standing centre stage wrestling with a change of recalcitrant clothes as the recital ground to an untimely halt. Rehearse such mundane matters!

As well as planning the mechanics carefully, make sure that the design element is not forgotten. At no time should the performance area resemble a junk shop. One candidate got over the need to store an unusually large number of props by putting them all into a trunk which in its turn was used as a platform for the dramatic text. The gist of these two paragraphs is that organisation and imagination are important twin facets of your presentation. Whatever you use in the course of the recital – use it well. It can mar as well as make.

THE TEXT FOR THE EXAMINERS

Please provide each of the two examiners with a clearly typed text. In this, in addition to the titles, indicate who wrote each of the selections and where they may be found. There is no need to give the link material which you will use as it is assumed that there is a degree of spontaneity about this. Some candidates decide to leave the programme with the examiner as a souvenir of the recital and this is a pleasant momento of the occasion, whatever the eventual result may be.

PRE-EXAMINATION PRESENTATIONS OF THE RECITAL

Seize whatever opportunities you are given to present the recital before the examination. This not only accustoms you to an audience, it also helps you to pace the work to get the best response from the people with whom you are communicating. Here are some possibilities:

- contact the Head of Drama or English at a nearby secondary or tertiary school and see if one of the senior classes would welcome the recital

- provided you give enough notice, local literary and local history groups also welcome appropriate recitals and the fairly short length of your own would allow time for an interesting discussion after the presentation

- day centres for the elderly or incapacitated, young wives groups, the Mothers' Union, Rotary and Round Table all provide a platform. Don't be afraid to approach people with an offer of your work: usually this is welcomed and if it is not convenient to the establishment to invite you, a refusal is quite painless!

- some candidates like to perform the recital either whole or in part at a local speech and drama festival. This is fine as long as you remember that the conditions of performance are very different to those in the examination room and that the scale of marking is often more generous (a matter of encouragement) than in an examination

CROSS REFERENCE

Many of the points I have made in the previous chapter about the recital at Medal stage also apply here, especially what I have said about marks and remarks.

ENVOI

It only remains for me to wish you a very enjoyable preparation for your examination and an interesting time during your performance. If you are of a suitable standard you will *earn* your medal or diploma; it will not be a matter of luck. But remember, this will be an award for your successful performance on a certain day. If you are going to make further progress as a performer on the other days, because he who stands still moves backwards, this is not the end of the journey – just the beginning!

INDEX